Nelie Chisolm.

THE

Chisolm Massacre:

A PICTURE OF

"Home Rule" in Mississippi.

BY JAMES M. WELLS.

NEGRO UNIVERSITIES PRESS
NEW YORK

Originally published in 1877
by Agency Chisolm Monumental Fund, Chicago

Reprinted 1969 by
Negro Universities Press
A DIVISION OF GREENWOOD PUBLISHING CORP.
NEW YORK

SBN 8371-1285-0

TO EMILY S. M. CHISOLM,

THE FAITHFUL WIFE, FOND MOTHER AND DEVOTED FRIEND,

WHOSE BITTER TEARS,

LIKE THE BLOOD OF HER MARTYRED AND BELOVED DEAD,

FALL TO THE EARTH AND PASS FROM SIGHT

UNHEEDED AND UNAVENGED,

THESE PAGES ARE AFFECTIONATELY INSCRIBED.

INTRODUCTION.

On Sunday, the twenty-ninth of April, 1877, a body of three hundred men, styling themselves "the best citizens" of Kemper county, in the State of Mississippi, conspiring together and co-operating with the sheriff and other officers of the county, coolly and premeditatedly murdered three men and two children; one of the latter a young and beautiful girl, and the other a delicate boy aged thirteen years. Against this act humanity itself, where humanity finds lodgment in the breasts of men, still cries out for vengeance; and the withering condemnation of an outraged public sentiment is everywhere turned upon the whole people of a State who stand supinely by, dumb and immovable spectators of such a crime without so much as a *pretended* effort toward the enforcement of the law against its perpetrators.

The inability of the courts of the country to arrest or punish is now admitted, and it is sought to palliate and justify the offense by invading the forbidden and hallowed precincts of the grave, and assailing the characters of the victims whose voices are hushed in the unbroken sleep of death. In behalf of justice to the living or dead, the laws of the land and the wail of the widow and orphan are alike unavailing.

Having been providentially called to witness this atrocity and its results, in their worst form and aspect, and knowing much of the men whose hands were employed in the bloody work, as well as of the causes which prompted them to its enactment; and, above all, being thoroughly acquainted with the lives and characters of the victims and the circumstances surrounding those who are left to mourn their untimely and terrible death, a sense of a solemn and imperative duty has impelled the author to undertake the difficult task which has resulted in the production of these pages. Nor has this been done with the hope of reward or fear of condemnation from any political organization or other source. The book is a simple record of facts, and for whatever there may be in them calculated to win plaudits from one or incur the displeasure of another the writer is in no way responsible. In their preparation, however, the necessity of producing something more than a simple and unqualified statement by which to establish the authenticity of the subject treated has been kept steadily in view, and where the circumstances seemed in any way to require it, some data or tangible proof of the correctness of every assertion made has been given, and the time, place and manner of its occurrence fixed.

The facts, dating back as far as 1870, are gleaned from personal observation of the author, whose business, carrying him into different parts of the State, has been of such a nature as to lead to a close investigation of the moral, social and political status and conduct of the people. The past four years, living in a county adjoining that of Kemper, which he has visited regularly and often, he has been made acquainted from time to time with the men and things here discussed.

With regard to the existence of the conspiracy to murder Judge Chisolm and his associates—which had its beginning soon after the close of the war, and culminated only when the last sod of earth was placed upon the grave of the faithful and heroic daughter, Cornelia— the circumstances of the murder itself, the subsequent treatment of the wounded, their sufferings and the manner of their death and burial, the writer is indebted to his own eyes, to the death-bed declarations of Judge Chisolm, and to the story as it came from the pale lips of the martyred girl, while the angels stood waiting to waft her spirit above. To all this is added the sworn testimony of more than twenty unimpeachable witnesses now living, whose names for their safety only are as yet withheld.

This evidence was taken by order of Attorney-General Devens, at the instance or demand of the British Minister at Washington, and was done for the purpose of ascertaining the facts with regard to the citizenship and death of Angus McLellan, the alleged British subject, one of the victims of the slaughter. To make this work complete and reliable, a special agent—Mr. G. K. Chase —was sent from Washington to co-operate with U. S. District-Attorney Lea, of Jackson, Mississippi, and these gentlemen, in company with Gen. Geo. C. McKee, of Jackson, and the writer, visited Meridian and De Kalb, where the facts were obtained, in strict accordance with which these pages are written. The coolness and deliberation of the plot to entrap the victims under a hollow pretense of executing the law, and then to murder them in cold blood; the shooting of Gilmer and McLellan on the streets and the assault of the mob upon the jail soon after; the murder of the little boy Johnny by Rosser, the leader of the savage horde, and the terrible vengeance visited upon the assassin's head by Judge Chisolm; the heroic defense of the father by the brave girl, and the patient suffering of the wounded through all the days that followed the dark Sabbath, till death came to their relief; all taken together afford a theme well calculated to enliven the fancy of a writer of the most extravagant tale of fiction, and cannot fail to arouse the sympathy and indignation of every honest heart throughout the world where the facts are known. A reproach to the civilization of the century in which we live, the cheek of · every true lover of all that is worthy of adoration in woman will mantle with shame when a record of this horror shall desecrate the pages which perpetuate the memory of a boasted chivalry, and American manhood must deny its name and existence so long as the blood of Cornelia and Johnny Chisolm is unavenged.

> " And do we dream we hear
> The far, low cry of fear,
> Where in the Southern land
> The masked barbaric band,
> Under the covert night,
> Still fight the coward's fight,
> Still strike the assassin's blow—

Smite childhood, girlhood low!
Great Justice! canst thou see
Unmoved that such things be?
See murderers go free,
Unsought? Bruised in her grave
The girl who fought to save
Brother and sire. She died for man.
She leads the lofty van
Of hero women. Lift her name
With ever-kindling fame.
Her youth's consummate flower
Took on the exalted dower
Of martyrdom. And death
And love put on her crown
Of high renown. * * * *
Cease, bells of freedom, cease!
Hush, happy songs of peace!
If such things yet may be,
Sweet land of liberty,
In thee, in thee!"

As a guarantee of the high character and responsibility of this work, and to show the object for which it is offered for sale, the following letter from Mrs. Chisolm is appended:

DeKalb, Mississippi, October, 1877.
To my kind friends and sympathizers :
Mr. James M. Wells, who has resided in Mississippi for the past nine years, where he has won the confidence and esteem of all with whom he has been associated, and who is known to me as a gentleman of high culture and strict personal integrity, has written a complete and reliable history of the late "Kemper County Tragedy," in

which my dear husband and children, with others of our friends, were foully and cruelly murdered.

Captain Wells was among the first to come to the aid of our suffering family after they were wounded, and kindly, skillfully and faithfully nursed them until death came to their relief, and he is in every way qualified for the task so generously undertaken.

The manuscript of the forthcoming work has been carefully perused by me, and meets my hearty approval.

At the solicitation of my friends at home and abroad the proceeds of the sale of this book will be devoted to the purpose of removing the bodies of my dear ones to some Northern State, beyond the reach of the desecrating hand of their enemies, where my home will hereafter be made, and there to erect a suitable monument to the memory of the martyred dead.

Captain Wells is fully empowered to transact all business incident to the publication and sale of the book, and is now in the city of Chicago, where his time and talent will be given to that end; and I earnestly commend him and the work he has in hand to the entire confidence of all who may desire the success of this generous undertaking; and any aid thus rendered him will be most gratefully and thankfully received, and treasured up in my heart, as the many acts of known and unknown friends have already been.

Gratefully and respectfully,

EMILY S. M. CHISOLM.

CONTENTS.

The Chisolm Massacre;

A PICTURE OF

"HOME RULE" IN MISSISSIPPI.

CHAPTER I.

William Wallace Chisolm, a sketch of whose eventful life and late tragic death will form, perhaps, the most important feature in the progress of this work, was born in Morgan county, Georgia, December 6th, 1830. At the age of sixteen years, together with his parents, he became a resident of Kemper county, Mississippi, a country which, then as now, was infested with great numbers of wicked and lawless men, the records of whose bloody crimes are still fresh in the memory of many of Kemper's oldest and most respected citizens. So marked was the spirit of violence and so light the regard for human life that the growth and improvement of the country was very slow; a condition which has followed its fortunes up to the present time. The accession of sober, industrious and trustworthy families to a community like that of Kemper, in those days, was welcomed and hailed with delight by all good people far and near, and the Chisolm family were not long in establishing their claim upon the latter class, where they ever after took rank among the first.

In the month of March, 1851, the head of the family died, leaving William—then a boy nineteen years old—its guardian and protector. Three of the children were younger sisters, and on his death-bed the father exacted of the son the promise that he would discharge all obligations of the estate, which amounted to a large sum for those early times and primitive surroundings, and that he would also educate the three sisters and provide for them comfortably in life. To the faithful performance of this duty young Chisolm at once set himself at work. How well he carried out this pledge the creditors or their heirs, and two of the sisters in good homes, surrounded by happy families, are still living to attest, while the mother, now at the ripe old age of seventy-four years, is provided with a neat cottage, situated on a farm which yields her a bountiful support, and that within sight of her early home in Mississippi, where all her children were reared and around which the survivors and their descendants are clustered to-day, if not *happy*, certainly *honored* and *revered*.

The 29th of March, 1856, the subject of this sketch was married to Emily S. Mann, an accomplished young lady, a daughter of John W. Mann, who was a native of Amelia Island, Florida, a prominent lawyer and a gentleman of high literary and social culture. The career of the Manns, in the early settlement of Florida, was somewhat remarkable. The grandfather of Emily S. Mann, who owned a large tract of land under

a Spanish grant, was the first settler, and built the
first house where the city of Fernandina now stands.
In the dispute between the early American settlers
in Florida and the Spanish authorities, in which the
former sought to take from Spain the lands claimed
by that government, the Manns, among others, took
prominent part, and by virtue of superior intelligence,
skill and bravery soon rose to distinction. These settlers were, many of them, driven from their homes, while
others were put to death outright or carried off and
compelled to drag out a life of refined torture as prisoners in Moro Castle, Cuba. Whether the theory is
correct or not, it is one of the inherent elements of
human conjecture to credit and foster the belief that the
strong characteristics which may in any way distinguish
the conduct of individuals are sure to mark and mould, in
some degree, the fortunes of their lineal posterity. Perhaps the bold and venturesome spirit which characterized the lives of this family in generations past, when
the iron rule of Spain was laid heavily upon these early
settlers, has had its influence in shaping the remarkable
life and character of Emily Mann Chisolm.

The education acquired by young Chisolm, up to the
date of his marriage, was only such as could be gleaned
at odd times in the common schools of the country,
which were then very poor; but with the assistance of a
dutiful and fond wife, his acquirements were soon made
to equal the spirit of enterprise and just emulation
already settled upon his heart. This dates the beginning
of an eventful and prosperous life.

Full of vigor and manly strength, young Chisolm first entered upon the business of farming, almost the only legitimate pursuit then open to the young men of the country, most of whom preferred a life of idleness and debauch to one of uninterrupted toil.

The 30th of January, 1858, W. W. Chisolm, at a special election held for the purpose of filling a vacancy in the office of magistrate, was elected to that important and honorable position in the beat or township in which he lived.

It was on the eleventh of February, 1858, that Cornelia Josephine, the first fruit of the marriage of W. W. Chisolm and Emily S. Mann was born. The sublime character of this pure girl, who, nineteen years after, fell a victim of savage outlawry, and died while defending her father against the assault of a blood-thirsty mob, is worthy the emulation of America's most exalted womanhood. Her young life, yielded up on the altar of filial love, and devotion to those principles of justice and right, which ever inspired the hearts of parent and child alike, cannot have been given in vain. The lesson taught by her example will live on, after the generation and the spirit which prompted these inhuman acts shall have been forgotten or numbered with the things of the past. As time advances and the proud names of our country's noble women are recorded, that of Cornelia Chisolm will be written in golden letters on its brightest page.

From this slight digression, the reader is brought back to the historical events in the order of their occurrence, which enter into the ground-work of this narrative.

In October, 1858, at a general election, young Chisolm was again made the choice of the people of his district, who re-elected him Justice of the Peace for a term of two years, which time he served with honor and credit to himself and to the entire satisfaction of his constituency. At all events, so well were the duties of this office performed, that in November, 1860, he was made Probate Judge of the county, a place which he held almost uninterruptedly until the year 1867, when he resigned in favor of John McRea, who was appointed by the then Provisional Governor of the State. During the long term in which he held this important position, Judge Chisolm was elected three times, running against Judge Gill, an older man, and one said to have been, next to Judge Chisolm, the most popular ever elected to an office in the county.

In all these years in which he enjoyed the confidence of his countrymen to such a high degree, Judge Chisolm was a pronounced Union man of Whig proclivities, and an uncompromising enemy of the party which precipitated and hurled head-long upon the country the terrible consequences of the rebellion. When the tide of secession swept over Mississippi like a devouring flame, he, with thousands of others like himself, who shuddered at the thought, in an unguarded moment, through force and intimidation, cast a vote favoring the disruption of the Union, an act which it is known he regretted all the remainder of his life. As a civil officer and citizen he was always opposed to the fratricidal contest, to which he steadily refused to lend any personal service, and never entered the army save only in the thirty days militia, and then under protest. The popular voice of the county, in the meantime, was in favor of a vigorous prosecution of the war, even unto the "last ditch."

Against all these odds Judge Chisolm was continued in office, from term to term, Whig and Unionist as he was.

Young and inexperienced in politics, there must have been in him, from the beginning, something which won the hearts of his fellows and called around him the elements of his unbounded success. At the close of the great struggle, he was among the few Southern men who early declared themselves in favor of reconstruction and the principles of the dominant party of that day, and to which he ever after adhered with a steadfastness and zeal amounting to patriotic devotion. Such were the leading characteristics of Judge Chisolm in youth and early manhood, and which gathered strength as time and age advanced, and through life marked the conduct of his public and private career.

Through an acquaintance with the people of Kemper county, as they were found in an early day, before the spirit engendered by rebellion could have had anything to do in moulding Southern character, the reader will be enabled more clearly to comprehend the peculiar state of morals which is found to have existed among them in later years; and which it must be believed was the natural outgrowth of a long-neglected and depraved condition of society. To make this point clear, the two following chapters are written. That there were then, as now, many good and true men and women living in this wild and unreclaimed region cannot be doubted, and they have nothing to fear from this record. To them every meed of praise is given, and should the eyes of any such chance to meet these pages, it must be borne in mind that only "the wicked flee when no man pursueth."

CHAPTER II.

For many years before the war and at its close, Kemper county, if not the whole State of Mississippi, might well have been included with Kentucky in her historic designation of "the dark and bloody ground;" for its population was, to a great extent, made up from a class of men who disregarded alike the laws of God and man, and "upon whom the multiplied villanies of nature swarmed in unwonted profusion." But unlike Kentucky, the deeds of barbarity committed within the borders of Kemper were not chargeable upon the untutored red man. None but the pure Anglo-Saxon race, and those to the manor born, were in any way responsible for the facts which are here recorded. Against this class, the efforts of the better citizens were often powerless and futile; and the officers entrusted with the execution of the law, either did not have the ability or were wanting in the disposition to arrest and punish.

In the little town of Narkeeta, in the year 1837, there was a tavern kept by one Geo. Capers, and a grog shop which was presided over by a rare genius named Nicholas Caton. The courts of the country at that time had very little influence in controlling the actions of men, as the judge, the sheriff or the juries were sure to have friends on one side or the other of the question to be settled; hence brute force became the only arbiter of peace. As a natural consequence of this, little neighborhood factions would spring up, hold brief but absolute sway for a day, or a month, and then as quickly give way to the temporary rule of another, which had proved itself more valiant in the use of the pistol or knife. For many years at Narkeeta there were two parties of the kind described, which alternated in the brief establishment of their authority, sometimes extending all over the county. These were led by the Doughtys on one side and the McLeans on the other. Horse racing, rapine, robbery and murder were of almost weekly if not daily occurrence throughout that and other sections. It is impossible, at this time to furnish the details of all the diabolisms that were then and there witnessed, as they would furnish a record of crime containing volumes. Only the most aggravated case, the details of which are still fresh in the memory of Narkeeta's oldest citizens, is here recounted. It will be sufficient to say, that from the year 1837 to 1842, there were committed, in the neighborhood spoken of, eighteen murders, the most diabolical of which occurred in the year 1839; in which George Capers waylaid and shot Nicholas Caton by the roadside. Caton, it appears, was apprised of his danger, and fearing death from a concealed enemy, while making a short journey through the country on horse-back, took up before him on the saddle a little child, eighteen months old, believing that its tender years and innocent prattle would form a temporary safeguard against the assassin's bullet. But in those days, as has been proved in more modern times, the presence of childhood had no power or influence in staying the hand of violence.

While passing through a thicket, Caton was shot from his horse and fell to the ground dead, still clasping in his arms the innocent child.

In the early spring of 1860, Adam Calvert had on his place two colored boys, the property of some heirs for whom a Mrs. Davis was guardian. The negroes, when hired to Calvert, had just recovered from an attack of measles. Mrs. Davis stipulated in the contract, before letting them go, that they should be subjected to no unnecessary exposure to the weather.

Ferguson, Calvert's overseer, a man of low instincts and beastial habits, had these two boys at work hauling rails, one day in the early spring, when there came up a very heavy and driving rain. Ferguson himself repaired to a shelter, leaving the injunction with one of the lads that if he should stop his team to take shelter from the rain it would be done at the peril of his life. But the storm came thicker and faster, and the poor fellow, chilled, benumbed and blinded, took refuge, for a few moments, under a large tree near by. When the rain had passed, Ferguson gave him a terrible beating, and left him with the promise that he would renew the punishment on the following day. The boy, then suffering from a raging fever, fearing that Ferguson would kill him, ran back to his mistress, Mrs. Davis, to whom he told the story of the cruel treatment he had received. It will be borne in mind that the penalty for harboring, or in any way aiding a runaway slave, was very severe; and, although Mrs. Davis' heart bled for him, she was compelled to send the boy back, with a note to Mr. Calvert, asking him not to inflict too severe punishment, and not any until he should recover from his fever.   Mr. Calvert, it appears, had gone from home that morning, and when the slave reached his place he handed the note to Mrs. Calvert.   Before sunrise of the next day Ferguson took him out behind a stable, stripped and tied him across a log, and, with a large rope, having knots tied in the end, whipped him in a most shocking and outrageous manner.   The victim's screams were heard by the neighbors living a mile and a half distant in every direction, and then to conclude, the brute jumped upon his back and stamped him with his coarse heavy boots.   On being released, it was found that the boy could not walk, and his brother, who was compelled to stand by and witness the scene, was ordered to carry him to the house, where he lingered in great agony until death came to his relief.   The brother then ran away, but was subsequently caught and the same treatment inflicted upon him; and, with the blood running from his wounds, he was lashed to a plow and made to follow it all day, without food or water.   Ferguson was never molested for this in any way.

Some five or six years before this, there was a man living near Scooba, who hired a negro child belonging to the McCaleb estate, and while having it in charge, whipped the child to death.   The people of the neighborhood were indignant at this outrage, and the murderer was compelled to *pay damages for the property thus destroyed.*

Years passed, and with them the spirit of outlawry increased, when men became, of a necessity, the more ready to take the law into their own hands. Such a thing as redress through the courts for any personal offense was rarely thought of. A man named Evret Roberts hired another to go to the house of Mr. McLawrin, against whom Roberts entertained a belief that he had been wronged, for the purpose of whipping him. McLawrin shot and killed his assailant. At another time, and on a pretext equally as trifling, John Edwards killed a man by the name of Eakins. Edwards' father, and his uncle, Jack Edwards, employed Mr. Simms, a lawyer, to go with them to examine some witnesses to the murder; but before arriving at the place of their destination, Jack Edwards — the uncle — shot and killed Simms. It appears they had had a difficulty before this, but were friendly at the time.

This terrible tragedy was soon followed by another, more appalling. A man named Tyson assaulted Mr. Spear with a hoe, while in a field at work. Spear was thus slain and his head beaten to a jelly. One of the Spears then killed a man by the name of Goins; stabbed him with a knife in the town of DeKalb. Satisfied with nothing short of a bloody vengeance, a brother of the murdered Goins, aided by a man named Diffey, killed Spear. They shot him from the bushes while Spear was at his supper.

At Blackwater, in Kemper county, George Alexander, a brother-in-law of one Phil Gully — whose character and name will be more fully discussed hereafter — had some words with Ben Caraway. They subsequently made friends, shook hands and separated; and from all civilized or savage usages of which we have any account one might suppose that further danger of assault by either party was at an end. But not so in Kemper. Caraway was a blacksmith, and went to work in his shop, little thinking of danger, when Alexander walked stealthily in, stepped up behind, and, at a single blow with a heavy piece of wood, struck him dead. For this murder—an unusual occurrence in cases of the kind— Alexander was arrested, placed under guard, and that night it is said Phil Gully procured his escape. Gully, on being asked if it would not have been better had Alexander been tried before leaving, replied that he thought not; he had taken counsel of Judge Hamm— then a practicing lawyer—and Hamm had told him that if tried, Alexander would certainly be hanged.

After the war closed there came from Alabama to Kemper county a young man named Jones, who first lived with a Mr. Madison, as a common laborer. Jones had had a difficulty with his step-father, in which he killed the latter in self-defense, and, to evade the vengeance threatened, fled to Mississippi. All this the young man very prudently kept to himself, remaining at his work, until one day, not many months after his arrival at Mr. Madison's he discovered a number of men riding up to the place, who inquired for a certain house in the neighborhood where they believed Jones to be. A man named Hal Dawson—of whom more will be said in another chapter—was at the head of this party, among whom the boy recognized the friends of his step-father, from Alabama. When these men had ridden away

Jones told a neighbor all about the trouble which had caused him to leave his home, and, knowing the desperate character of Dawson, he was advised to go at once to the home of his uncle, Mr. Mardis, who lived in the same county. In compliance with this suggestion he went, and while at his uncle's house, and before revealing to him the secret of his troubles, he again saw Hal Dawson ride up, in company with one Sloke Gully, a relative of Phil, the one alluded to on another page. Jones now told his uncle why he had left his home, and at once determined to go back, and accordingly started on foot for Alabama; but while on the road he lost his way and came out at Sloke Gully's house. Feeling hungry and not knowing who lived there, the young man asked for something to eat. This was given him, and while partaking, who should again appear but Dawson and Gully himself. On seeing them, Jones sprang from the table and ran down across a field, hotly pursued by Gully and Dawson. After he had reached the cover of the woods — still pursued — several shots were heard in that direction by the people who had been observing. In a few minutes Gully and Dawson returned, stating that they had been unable to overtake the object of their pursuit. A few weeks thereafter some ladies, when out walking, discovered the body of the murdered boy in the creek which runs near the place from whence the firing was heard.

Meantime Mr. Mardis, supposing his nephew had gone back to Alabama, said nothing of the matter, until one day some two months afterward, when in

DeKalb, he was accosted by John W. Gully, then sheriff, who told Mardis that he had better "go slow," adding at the same time, "there is catching before hanging, and you can't prove who killed young Jones."

It was before this that " Etna," a colored woman, was taken out by some unknown parties, tied to a tree and whipped to death. Her body was found there on the following day, in a perfectly nude state.

About the same time, a colored man named Moses McDade was found dead in the road. He had been wantonly shot by some parties unknown. A Baptist minister by the name of Henry White was present at the lynching and hanging of a negro for some alleged offense during the war, and lent material aid in the performance of the murderous act. He afterwards asserted that he was ready and more than willing to engage, at any time, in an undertaking of the kind when his *pastoral* duties did not interfere.

In the spring of 1865, James Johnson, a white man, was waylaid, when going from his home in the Southwest Beat, to DeKalb, shot and instantly killed. Johnson had been a merchant and was highly respected.

CHAPTER III

During all these years a family by the name of Gully—the same already mentioned—held almost undisputed control of the public patronage of Kemper county. From the Sheriff's office down to the Beat Magistrate and Constable, a Gully or some one of their immediate connections wore the official robes, carried the baton of authority and the keys of the exchequer. By free use of the jug and kindred influences, their election was secured from term to term, and when installed in office the courts and the juries were by them manipulated and controlled. So notorious had this become that it was a matter of common observation, as it was a fact, that unless a man could establish his relationship to the Gullys, or in some other way ingratiate himself into their favor, it was useless to look for political honors within the gift of the people of the county; but when this relationship was once established, a *carte blanche* for political promotion and immunity for any offense, however grave, was secured.

The first Sheriff of Kemper county defaulted and ran away. The second was "Sloke" Gully, the father of Phil, Henry, Sam, Jess and John W. The third Sheriff was James Hull, a Northern man, who came to Mississippi, in an early day, and married a Gully. Hull held the office for eight years and then vacated it to accept that of Circuit Clerk, which he held for sixteen years.

Phil Gully was the next in order, and became Hull's successor to the sheriff's office. "Old Sloke,"—as the father
was commonly called — politically was a Whig, and sometimes said that if heaven was to be governed by democrats he did not care to enter its pearly gates. Fortunately, as is believed, politics does not enter into the
conduct of affairs in that brighter world; besides it is
the opinion of those who know the Gullys best, that
their counsels will never be sought nor obtained there.
Phil was recreant to the early teachings of his father
and espoused the more popular cause of democracy, as
did all of his brothers. During Phil's administration
the people complained bitterly of the long-continued
reign of the Gully family. Notwithstanding this, by
sheer power of numbers and brute force, John W.
Gully became Phil's successor and held the office for
eight years, during which time the war came on. The
Gullys, although valiant in words, overbearing and aggressive when certain of their ability to surmount opposition,
were, in fact, non-combatant all through the memorable
struggle for their "most sacred rights." During that time
John W., himself exempt from military duty by virtue of
being sheriff, had fourteen different members of his family
appointed as deputies, which position also relieved them
from the hazardous responsibilities of a soldier. So
chronic was the desire of the Gullys for office, that while
the State was under Confederate management, Henry
and Phil became opposing candidates for the Legislature, and the contest between them is said to have been
like that when "Greek meets Greek." Only one of the

name—Henry—did any service in the army. John W. was what is familiarly termed in the South a "buttermilk" soldier—a home guard—a hero of thirty days' duration. His conduct in the department of his choice is said to have been "gallant," as was that of the whole command to which he belonged. A recent newspaper eulogium, written by Judge Foote of Macon, Mississippi—and who was Colonel of the "buttermilk brigade"—on the life and character of John W. Gully, assures the public that "Captain Gully gave him—the Colonel—very little trouble." Doubtless Gully, if living, could say as much for Foote. From this it will be seen that these two gentlemen must have "fought like brave men, long and well," in defense of their "fires." As it could not have been Gully's superior prowess as a soldier that gave him character and influence, the theory already advanced is the more easily understood; that, by close and intimate connection with the worst element of society, strengthened by the great numbers of his own family connection, he became the acknowledged leader of his clan; for certainly the "many virtues" usually claimed for men seeking the patronage of an indulgent public, were never found in this man, who for so many years controlled the political destinies of the county. He was coarse, vulgar and illiterate; ambitious, arrogant and overbearing, as will be seen; with a moral status which cannot be said to have been above reproach. The *soubriquet* familiarly applied to him, is in itself a very fair index to his character. Wherever known he bore the more appropriate than chaste appellation of the "Bull of the Woods."

So long had the Gully family and their adherents managed all public enterprises in the county where a pecuniary reward was made the chief incentive to action that, as might be supposed, they could but illy brook opposition, and terrible indeed must have been the jealousy and hatred which this clan bore toward the men who first had the hardihood and daring to "beard the lion in his den," and who were finally successful in loosing his strong grip. But year after year passed by, while the iron heel of the Gully rule became more and more irksome. It is told of Hull, while sheriff, that he would enter a man's house ostensibly for the purpose of serving some legal process, and then demand, by authority of his high office, any sum of money, no matter how exorbitant and unjust. These sums were frequently paid over to him, and one of the victims of this peculiar style of robbery is living in Kemper to-day, and who has kindly lent the weight of his experience in the establishment of these facts. Charges of corruption in office and crime out of it were almost continually being brought against one or another of this clan of public plunderers. As sheriff, the most unreasonable and unjust accounts were presented by Gully to a board of supervisors, generally under his control, many of which were by them allowed, and the money for the whole account finally wrenched from the poor taxpayer. Accounts of this kind, for extra services rendered and special deputies employed, have first to be approved by the presiding judge of the court and district attorney. When these gentlemen could not be conveniently

reached, Gully, it appears, was in the habit of affixing
their names to the bills himself.

Some years after, when John E. Chisolm—a brother
of Judge Chisolm—became sheriff by appointment of
the governor, a warrant thus fraudulently obtained,
amounting to two hundred and forty dollars—more or
less—was taken by Judge Chisolm, then performing the
duties of the office of sheriff for his brother, for taxes
due the county. But now that a man of a political
faith which they did not endorse had the handling of the
public funds, claims of every description presented
against the county underwent the most rigid examination by a democratic board of supervisors, and this
warrant, offered by Judge Chisolm, was rejected by
reason of the exorbitancy of the account on which it
was based, and other gross irregularities. One reason
assigned for this was, it had been taken by Judge Chisolm
at a discount, and that he now sought to turn it over, in
settlement for taxes, at its face. The judge called up
the man of whom he took the paper—Mr. John A.
Menese, who swore that he had been allowed its full
value. Upon further investigation it was found that the
original account itself was a forgery, as it had never been
approved by the presiding judge or district attorney.
At least the prosecuting officer, Mr. Thomas H. Wood,
declared at the time that the signing of his name to the
document was a forgery, and so it was rejected by
the board. Judge Chisolm's only recourse then was to
sue Gully for the amount, which he did, obtaining a
judgment against him accordingly. Gully appealed

and, for some error in the declaration, the supreme court remanded the case, where it remained unsettled until Gully's death.

With George Welch—the present deputy sheriff—as clerk of the court, and, by virtue of that office, clerk of the board of supervisors, some $1,900 in warrants thus fraudulently obtained were found, which the taxpayers were compelled to cash, and for which no satisfactory explanation has yet been made.

It is said that while sheriff of Kemper county after the war, John W. Gully turned over to the treasurer between two and three thousand dollars of old Confederate warrants, issued by the board of police—or supervisors—during the progress of the rebellion, and with them paid the county tax of 1866. One of the items was a warrant for $500, issued to him for collecting a military tax. This, with the balance, had been paid in Confederate money. These warrants were received by the treasurer on Gully's making oath that he had paid their face value. By this the crime of perjury was added to that of unlawfully taking the people's money. By the aid of his ring of Confederates he bought up warrants at twenty-five to forty cents on the dollar, and turned them over to the treasurer dollar for dollar, under oath that he had taken them for taxes, without discount. For three years following that of 1856 this man collected a sum of money due from the county to the Mobile & Ohio Railroad Company, amounting to $3,000, and which, up to the year 1870, at least, had not been given to that corporation; while the receipts for the money paid to Gully can be seen to-day. During this great and good administration of the people's affairs, many disgraceful acts and foul crimes not connected with his office were charged against him. The nature of these are such as to preclude the possibility of their publication in a work of this kind, and it is with pleasure that a further recital of this peculiar phase of Kemper county society is omitted.

In the spring of 1868 this man Gully, who had been ungovernable and rebellious toward the authorities placed over the State by the General Government, was removed from the office of sheriff, and A. H. Hopper, an ex-Confederate soldier and a native of Alabama, was appointed in his place. Benjamin F. Rush, who was also a Southern man of high personal character, and who had been a soldier of marked gallantry, was made Hopper's chief deputy.

On the accession of Hopper, county warrants were a drug in the market at twenty-five cents on the dollar, and bankruptcy and ruin stared the people in the face.

Before this, however, Rush had been associated with Gully and another gentleman in the mercantile business, during which time they quarreled, and Gully openly accused Rush of foul dealing, while Rush preferred counter charges against Gully. A personal difficulty, which appears to have been the only means of settling disputes of the kind, was the result, when Rush attacked Gully with a pistol, driving him within the cover of his house. From the date of this collision the war of crimination and re-crimination ceased between them, and they met again on terms of comparative friendship. It was not until Rush became the recipient of the emoluments of the sheriff's office, which had so long been an undisputed heritage of the Gullys, that a second rupture occurred between them.

From the date of the appointment of Hopper, Gully's persecution of Rush knew no rest, and, already leaning toward republicanism, the latter was soon driven into the ranks of that poor and despised party; while Chisolm, McRea, Hopper and one or two others, formed a nucleus around which a strong and effective organization sprung up.

This marked the beginning of a war of political persecution and proscription—somewhat local in its character, it is true—as cruel and unjust as the religious oppression of the Huguenots under the reign of Philip the Second of Spain, or that of Pedro Melendez in the early history of our country. What added fresh fuel to the flame of disappointed ambition, the colored man stepped forward with that most potent of all weapons in a political contest—the ballot—and rallied around the men who had been first to espouse the principles guaranteeing to them equal and exact rights under the law. Thus shorn of their power, the Gullys—most of them illiterate as the negroes themselves—first grew restive and then desperate as the vision of their former greatness began to fade. Like many others, they feigned the belief that the negro was soon to be made the equal, socially, morally and politically, of the proud Caucassian race, his "natural master." For it is a fact, and upon reflection the principle is readily understood, that the greater the ignorance and the lower the moral status of a white man reared in the South, the more bitter is his prejudice against the late slave, and the greater his fear that the despised race will eventually become the white man's equal in the common scale of humanity.

Up to this date, through all the years of Judge Chisolm's public career, he had been so well liked by the Gullys that at all times he received their earnest and hearty support; for without it he could not have been continued so long in one of the most honored offices within the gift of the people of the county, in which the political power and numerical strength of the Gullys was so great, and this fact is conceded by Gully's friends to-day. Aside from his individual merits, Judge Chisolm had growing up around him, at this time, an interesting and cultivated family. The early training of his accomplished wife, had peculiarly fitted her for that companionship so much needed by a man surrounded with the exciting and often demoralizing influences incident to and inseparable from public life; while, to her children, she was at once a true mother, a faithful tutor and an engaging companion, as well as a blessing to the society which she adorned.

Thus is outlined at the beginning the characters of the individuals whose life-record furnish much of the material upon which this truly remarkable narrative of facts is founded. Their relations to each other and the community in which they lived for so many years before the direful consequences of the civil war came upon the country, have been presented. The social and moral standing of each is truthfully given, and it will not require the closest attention in the progress of this work, to enable the reader to mark the causes of complaint as subsequently charged upon one by the other, and to discriminate between the false and the true. If a just discrimination should thus be arrived at, after reading, then the great object for which these pages are written will have been well-nigh accomplished; for to refute false charges made against the dead — and the living who are equally powerless for defense — charges given strength and currency through the agency of a partisan press, as incapable of truth in the discussion of any topic where political questions are in any way involved, as it is weak and imbecile upon all others, has been one of the chief inspirations of this work.

The 14th of September, 1869, John E. Chisolm, the same spoken of on a preceding page, who lived near the old family homestead, in a remote part of the county, was appointed by Governor Ames to succeed Hopper as sheriff; while Judge Chisolm — then ineligible on account of having served in a civil capacity under the Confederate government — was made his brother's deputy, and assumed the whole responsibility of the office.

Before the administration of John E. Chisolm, under the supervision of a democratic board of supervisors, a tax was levied upon the county which was known as the "acre tax," and against which there appeared, at the time of the levy, no especial objection; but when Judge

Chisolm undertook to colleet the tax there went up a terrible cry against the law which was characterized as a great "radical steal." No better explanation of this matter can be given than that found in the sworn testimony of Judge Chisolm before the Congressional Investigating Committee at Washington, February 14th, 1877, page 757, and but a few weeks before his cruel assassination.

In answer to a question by Mr. Teller, Judge Chisolm said: "There was a tax levied in 1869 by a democratic board of supervisors of the county for county purposes, levied upon land — upon the acres of land. One cent given in upon land at such a price, two cents upon land given in at another price, and three cents upon land given in at the highest price."

Question.—"Per acre?" *Answer.*—"Yes; the tax books were turned over to me, or rather to my brother (I was doing the collecting and was running the office; it was before my disabilities were removed), and a number of gentlemen asked me what I thought about the levy. I told them that it was not my business to decide any legal question; it was simply a matter to enjoin the sheriff about, or else to pay the tax; that the board of supervisors left no discretion with me. I had to collect the tax or be enjoined. A majority of the land owners of the county enjoined the sheriff from collecting the tax. Some paid the tax rather than enjoin. That tax was paid over to the county treasurer, and I got his receipt for it. I never heard any one make complaint about it except Esquire Mills, who was a kind of crazy man down there. He paid the tax, and then commenced a lawsuit against me for not paying it back to him. It was my duty, under the law, to pay it to the county treasurer."

Question. — " Did you pay it to the county treasurer ? " *Answer.* — " I did ; I paid it to the county treasurer. Mr. Mills commenced suit against the treasurer, and the circuit and superior courts both decided that I had done right in the premises."

And thus vanished in smoke the first specific charge of dishonesty ever preferred against Judge Chisolm by his malicious and vindictive enemies, seeking only to destroy the power and influence of the man who, of all others, now stood most in their way. Meantime the slanderous tongue of hatred spared neither age or sex, and the sanctity of republican homes was invaded when all other efforts failed to catch the quick ear of an ignorant rabble, whose passions and prejudices might thus be further excited against the men whose ruin had already become the chief goal of democratic ambition in the county. Gully once more took up the cudgel against Rush, pursued him with a keen scent, and all the venom of his nature. Unable to bear his taunts and insults longer, Rush, sometime in August, 1870, sent Gully word that he would attack him on sight. Gully armed himself with a gun, and in company with his brother, Sam, and a Dr. Smith, started down the street, in DeKalb, toward his home, on horseback. Rush saw the three men coming and approached them, with a gun in his hands, from an open square, in plain sight. Gully reined his horse across the street, bringing his brother and Smith between himself and Rush. Rush called out to him to stop—that he wanted to settle their difficulties then and there. At this, Sam Gully shot Rush with a pistol which he had previously drawn, and at the same moment seized Rush's gun, which went off in the struggle that followed. Upon this Smith fled for his life, and John Gully jumped from his horse, ran behind the nearest building and then turned and fired twice upon Rush, one shot taking effect, bringing him to the ground. At this time it was discovered that Sam Gully had been shot in the right leg, which, while sitting on his horse in the position he occupied when struggling with Rush, was on the side next to his brother John. Sam Gully died, from the effects of his injuries, that night. The evidence elicited before the grand jury was to the effect that a shot from Rush's gun, at the time, could not have inflicted the wound that caused Gully's death. Notwithstanding this fact, an indictment was found; but it is believed, to this day, by all who have gone into an impartial investigation of the subject, that John Gully, in shooting at Rush, accidently shot and killed his own brother. Rush was carried home, and lingered for days and weeks at the point of death. His trial was afterward had in the circuit court for the killing of Sam Gully, and he was acquitted. John W. Gully stood trial for the shooting of Rush, and was also acquitted. After the trial of these men, the decision of the public seemed to be that honors were now easy, and in all probability, there would be no more personal collisions between them.

But in this they were mistaken, for Gully proved to be as vindictive and untiring in the pursuit of an enemy, as he was arrogant and ambitious of political power and distinction, and Rush had no sooner recovered from the effects of his wounds, and entered upon his accustomed avocation, than Gully renewed his attack, but this time in an entirely new and unlooked-for manner. Rush had always been open, bold, and when driven to the wall, aggressive. All through the war, while Gully was screening himself and his relations from the rigors and hazards of the tented field, Rush stood without a peer in everything that went to make up the gallant soldier. His public and private record was without a blemish, and no one believed that he could have had an enemy so cowardly and mendacious as to undertake to assassinate him in cold blood; and certain it is that no one but a Gully has ever been accused of that crime.

In the month of March, following this disastrous collision, in August an attempt was made to assassinate Rush, which came very near proving a success. He was shot from behind a church—a singularly chosen place to screen an assassin—which stands just across the street, opposite his house, while going into his gate, after dark. The best idea, perhaps, of how this attempt to murder was brought about, and by whom, can be gleaned from the testimony of Judge Chisolm, as taken before the Joint Select Committee of Congress of 1871, appointed to inquire into the condition of affairs in the late insurrectionary States.

On page 247 of the official report will be found the

following: In answer to a question by Mr. Poland,
the chairman, Judge Chisolm said:

"I was the first man who got to Rush's after he was
shot; was at the court house when I heard the shots.
We were trying to secure a person at the time Captain
Rush left the court house. I had seen a great deal of
maneuvering going on among men whom I regarded as
very bad men in the community. Just at dark I told
Captain Rush that I thought he had better look out,
that I thought there was going to be another raid in the
county, that I saw some maneuvering going on that I
did not like. I told him that I thought we had better
do all we could to the jail and get back home before
dark. There was a man by the name of Hunger in jail
for housebreaking. He came near escaping two or three
times. He seemed to be a very powerful man. Captain
Rush said to me just as he left, 'Judge, you stay here
until the workman has done all he can do to the jail, and
I will go home, for I do not feel well.' His house was
perhaps seventy-five yards from the jail. Rush was my
deputy, and had charge of the jail."

Question.—"You said you had discovered some suspicious movements, then, that day?" *Answer.*—"Yes, sir;
and I had informed Rush and three others there, that
evening, that there was something wrong going on; that
the men who had concocted bloody schemes before were
concocting them again, and I requested three different
men to have their guns ready for a night's fight if it was
found necessary to make it. These movements con-
sisted mainly of seeing a number of men collected

in the back of Gully's store — a gentlemen there whom I think every man in the county, irrespective of party, regards as one who does not care anything about having the law executed. There were several men there from out in the country; two of them brothers of this man Gully, and several other suspicious characters. There was one other man in town whom I did not know at all."

Question. — "Why did you suspect these men of hostility toward Rush?" *Answer.* — "I suspected them of hostility toward any man who was opposed to lawlessness, and rioting, and doing things illegal and wrong in the county; more especially to Rush, because he and they were not friendly, as these parties are not friendly to any man who does not agree with them in politics. Captain Rush was a republican and the others were democrats. Rush was very badly wounded. The middle finger of his right hand was shot off, and he was shot through the groin and through the abdomen; but the bullets did not go to the hollow. Four shots struck him; but his pocketbook and knife turned them, and I think saved his life. His right hand was in his pocket when he was shot. He was shot twice with a double-barrel gun. He was about ten steps from his gate when the first shot was fired at him. He then made a spring for his gate, when they fired at him again. It was the first shot that hurt him worst. When they fired at him the second time some of the shots went into the house, and came very near killing his wife."

CHAPTER IV.

Years have passed since the government emerged from a life struggle scarcely equalled in the history of nations. Old land marks are lost sight of, the statute books of the country changed, and the constitution of the fathers has been remodeled and placed upon a higher plane of justice and humanity. But civil convulsions or the visitations of Providence, no matter how sudden and terrifying, do not always appeal to the reason or conscience. The wicked hearts of men are slow to change, and in Mississippi, in 1866, are found the same discordant and turbulent elements which existed there in 1836.

The caldron of political rancor had now been raised to a boiling heat throughout Mississippi, and the hand of persecution and the ban of social ostracism fell heavily upon every one who dared to express an opinion that was not first entertained by the leaders of the old secession party. Ku-Klux organizations existed in a majority of the counties, while those not so fortunate as to possess a safe-guard of the kind, had only to despatch couriers to adjoining counties, or even States, when an emergency seemed to demand it, and before the sun rose on the day following the despatch fifty or a hundred mounted and masked men would appear ready for the execution of any crime, no matter how cowardly and dark. The system of free schools, which had been established in the State, seemed to be one of the

W. W. Chisolm

strongest incentives to the development of the Ku-Klux spirit, and the whipping of teachers, the killing of negroes and burning of school houses, proved an occupation in which they took special delight. It is hardly necessary here to undertake to impress upon the reader the magnitude of this great evil, which extended all over the southern States. Its history is well known, and the subject is alluded to only as a link in the continued chain of events. The estimate placed upon the education of the youth of the State in ante-bellum times, and the care taken of the funds donated by the General Government for that purpose, will throw a light upon this subject not generally understood. It will account in some degree, perhaps, for that hostility claimed to have existed against the inauguration of the free school system in the State; and it will strengthen the evidence already adduced, tending to show the outlawed condition of society wherever republican institutions were sought to be introduced and maintained. By the twelfth section of the Act of Congress of March 3, 1803, regulating the grant and disposal of lands south of the Tennessee, the section number sixteen in each township, "is reserved for the support of public schools in the same." Mississippi received a large proportion of this grant. The report of Hon. H. R. Pease, State Superintendent of Public Education for the year 1870, which is in part reproduced, will show the condition in which this fund was found at the close of the war. Here are the reports of the various superintendents of the counties:

In Claiborne county: "The work of ascertaining the

exact condition of the school lands was very much retarded on account of the loose manner in which the business has heretofore been done. With regard to the claims due the school fund, the amounts 'regarded as worthless,' are worthless indeed. Some are against persons that are dead, and have left no estate, or one covered up by judgments; some are against persons who have bankrupted against them, and a few are barred by limitation. I think much of the above funds could have been saved if the President of the Board of Police had taken steps to secure it, as required by an Act of the Legislature, approved December 2, 1865, and entitled 'An Act the better to secure the payment of the School Funds of the State.' See Acts of 1865, Chapter 20. Of the amounts 'regarded as good,' there may and probably will be some considerable loss when the solvency of the debtors is tested in court."

In Clarke county : " Sometime has been spent in investigating the condition of the Sixteenth Section Fund and all school moneys. The old records of this county have been so badly kept, that no satisfactory results have been obtained."

In Tallahatchie county: " Prominent amongst the difficulties we have been called upon to encounter, is the fierce opposition of the white people to paying taxes for the establishment and support of colored schools, for 'ruining and demoralizing the negro.' This prejudice, bitter and uncompromising, has deterred many applicants for certificates from accepting colored schools. The party recently appointed to the office of treasurer of the county is known as an open and uncompromising enemy of public schools, and he has informed applicants for certificates that they would not be paid, as there was no money in the treasury, and that the tax levied for 'Teachers' Fund' would be paid in depreciated county paper."

In Yazoo county: "At this date, February 9, 1871, there are in operation, under the free system, forty-one schools in this county. We find it impossible to get at a correct estimate of the 'Common School Fund.' The ante-bellum claims are in such a fix that but little will be realized from them. Bankruptcy, death and emigration has destroyed all hopes of getting the most of them. Many of the papers are either destroyed or mislaid. Some thirty-six thousand dollars of this fund was invested in the Mississippi Central Railroad stock, some twelve or fifteen years ago. The 'Sixteenth Section Fund' is in a very bad condition, so much so that nothing approaching accuracy can be stated."

In Kemper county: "When organized, my Board of School Directors went to work looking after the notes, books and papers due the several townships, for the proceeds of sale of Sixteenth Section lands, which were turned over to Esquire A. G. Ellis for collection. I cannot give you a definite answer as to the condition of these claims; but am of opinion that *about half* of them may be considered good. * * * We have several school houses free of rent, and with the exception of two sub-districts, the people have built their own school houses, and all seem satisfied; except, however,

the disappointed party—the revolutionists or seces-
sionists. They are not satisfied, and would not be at
anything, be it to their interest ever so much. We have
now between forty and fifty schools, with good teachers,
organized and in a flourishing condition. I adopted in
the outset the prerequisite 'that no teacher should be
employed unless indorsed by the parents and guardians
of the neighborhood in which he or she proposed to
teach.'"

In Franklin county: "I have made every effort to
obtain from the old school officers the notes *which were*
in their possession, showing the disposition which has
been made by them of these funds, and the indebtedness
of parties to whom the funds have been loaned. Many
of these notes I find to be against persons who are now
insolvent, and many are barred by limitation."

In Jackson county: "Most of the records were
destroyed by fire during the year 1862, and lately the
minute book of the board of police has been spirited
away by some unknown party."

In Neshoba county: "I have heretofore informed the
State Board of Education that the school lands of
the county, known as the Sixteenth Section Lands, were
nearly all disposed of by lease or otherwise many years
ago, and that the proceeds arising from the leasing of
the same have been so managed, both during and since
the war, that *they are at this time almost entirely worthless*. The aggregate amount of school funds on out-
standing claims is $18,738.73; one-half of the above
amount secured by very doubtful paper, and in a manner
worthless."

In Prentiss county: "We labor under another disadvantage, which perhaps is not general. The ignorance among the people in the rural districts here is absolutely astounding. Indeed in some localities they seem to need missionaries to teach them civilization more than school teachers."

To conclude, Superintendent Pease himself subjoins the following:

"Over thirty buildings, used for school purposes, have been destroyed by mobs or burned by incendiaries in the past year. The following extract from an official report received at this office, will exhibit the character of hostility manifested in certain localities of the State: *   *

'Duty once more prompts me to inform you what has transpired in relation to the public schools of the county since my last communication upon this subject. There have been four school houses burned since my last report, two of which were used for white pupils and the other two for the colored children. We do not know whether these outrages were committed by private parties or by the Ku-Klux. The town of Louisville was visited, a few nights ago, by some thirty-six or seven disguised horsemen. They went to the residence of Mr. Fox, an honorable and well known gentleman, who was engaged in teaching a public school, and forbade him further complying with the contract made with the Board of Directors. They then went in search of one Peter Cooper, a colored man, employed in teaching a colored school, and failing to find his person, they sought revenge in destroying his property. They burned his trunk, together with the most of his clothing, also destroyed or carried off twenty-six dollars in money. They then called on two others, using the lash pretty freely, then departed to parts to us unknown. They have notified a good many of the teachers to stop teaching public free schools in the county, some of whom have obeyed their command. There have been, by burning and otherwise, eleven public schools stopped in the county. They seem determined to break up all the schools in the county.' Many instances of a similar character, in the eastern counties, have been reported. I will state to your honorable body, in reply to your resolution requiring the location of the school buildings destroyed, that I am unable to report the exact location, as the reports from which my statement is taken simply give the numbers, without giving the exact location. I have taken steps to secure this information, and will, if required by competent authority, furnish the same, accompanied by affidavits setting forth the facts.

" From the reports received up to date, I am able to present the following results. I will add, in this connection, that these figures exhibit the result of a preliminary investigation only :

Amount of loss in loans for want of proper
security, ... $61,660 00
Amount of loss in rents of school lands, . 58,960 00
Number of acres of school lands occupied for
which no rent has been paid, ... 16,018 00
Total amount of loss of school lands on
account of·neglect and want of proper
management on the part of former school
officers, ... 402,729 00

" I am of the opinion that when full and complete returns are made of the amount of loss of the sixteenth section school funds alone, to say nothing of the seminary fund, and the Chickasaw fund, will exceed ONE MILLION OF DOLLARS absolutely squandered and irretrievably lost."

In Kemper county the spirit of blood-thirsty intolerance toward the negro and his " white allies," as all white republicans were called, became so great, and murders and whippings by the Ku-Klux so alarmingly frequent, that troops were finally called in and a military camp was established at Lauderdale Springs, the most accessible point on the Mobile and Ohio Railroad. Among the nightly raiders upon the unoffending blacks of Kemper county there came up at this period a special genius named Ball. He was arrested by the military and carried to Lauderdale, charged with murder. He subsequently made his escape and fled, as is believed to Texas. So aggravating was this case that a large reward was offered for Ball's apprehension. But a few months passed before he secretly returned; yet strange to tell, did not ally himself with his old associates in blood. This strange conduct aroused a suspicion in the minds of his former confederates that he was about to turn State's evidence and expose all their iniquities. At any rate, one dark night his house was surrounded by some unknown parties and several shots fired into it, in precisely the same manner in which Ball himself, with his masked brethren, had so often fired into the cabins of defenseless negroes. His guilty and cowardly heart doubtless revealed to him the terrible truth that, whoever his assailants might be, their purpose was to avenge the blood for which his own hands were accountable, and under cover of the thick darkness he sought to escape by flight; but was finally shot down, receiving wounds from which he died in a few days. This occurred near the house of Phil Gully; though whatever else may be said of him, it was not then believed Gully would willingly imbue his hands in blood. But at that time, as to-day, it was asserted by Judge Chisolm's friends that he planned Ball's murder and was fully cognizant of every other murder committed by the Klan, that he furnished the brains for maturing their plans and carrying them into successful execution, under the personal supervision of John W. Gully, his brother. At the instance of Phil Gully two negroes were arrested, charged with the killing of Ball. There being no jail or other suitable place for the confinement of prisoners, one of them escaped, while the other stood a trial and was honorably acquitted.

Ball's depredations, however, were not always done under the cover of night or the black mask; nor were they yet confined to the colored race. Some time before Ball's death Judge Chisolm had been deputized to collect some taxes in the southwestern portion of the county, and when returning, with a large amount of money on his person, he encountered Ball in a dense swamp at the crossing of a creek. This was near Phil Gully's house. Ball placed himself in the road with a' double-barrel gun, and demanded of Judge

Chisolm if he intended to arrest him or expose his whereabouts to the military authorities.

The Judge replied that he was not himself an officer, and had no authority to arrest any one. Peering into the thicket near by, Chisolm then discovered that Ball was not alone; for there, ·crouched in the brush, with guns in their hands, he saw a half dozen other men. The Judge was in a defenseless condition, having no arms on his person but a small pistol. While talking with Ball and assuring him that he would not inform on nor undertake to arrest him, Judge Chisolm rode away and escaped without injury.

The night of the 26th of May, 1871, a body of disguised men visited the plantation of ex-Governor R. C. Powers, for the purpose of killing a colored man who lived there at the time. The superintendent on the place—a white man—refused them admission to the room where the object of their search was sleeping. Upon this they opened fire upon the cabin with their guns, two balls passing through the door in which the young man stood when disputing their entrance. This was followed by a personal assault upon the door, which was soon beaten down; but, during that time, one of the assailants fell dead from a shot delivered by the superintendent, who, with the negro, then fled for his life. They were followed by several shots which did no harm, when the would-be murderers, taking up the dead body of their fallen comrade, hurried away, but in their haste and consternation, left behind them two Ku-Klux masks, which had accidentally fallen off. George Evans, the young man

killed, had been raised in the county, and was well known
by everybody. Two of his brothers were arrested by the
military previous to this, charged with killing a freedman.
Evans' body was buried secretly, on his father's place,
early the next morning, and the report was circulated
that he had died suddenly of cholera morbus. His
father said that his death was caused from eating too
many oysters and sardines the night before. The kind
of which he partook was unhealthy, no doubt.

The immediate occasion of this visit of the Klan to
the plantation of ex-Governor Powers, was as follows:
Matt Duncan, the colored man whom they sought to
kill that night, some two years before had reported to the
military, at camp Lauderdale, the murder of a little
brother of his by the same crowd of men. This boy —
Matt's brother — was taken from his cabin, drawn and
quartered and his mangled body thrown into the Talla-
dega swamp. Matt's offense was that of reporting this
"little act of pleasantry" to the authorities. He was a
hard-working and industrious negro, and seldom quit the
place for any purpose.

This is the sworn testimony of ex-Governor Powers,
as taken before the investigating committee of Congress
in 1871. The ex-Governor lives in Mississippi to-day,
and his testimony will hardly be impeached.

During all these years of outlawry, unequaled in the
history of barbarous tribes anywhere on the earth,
according to the sworn testimony of Judge Chisolm, the
headquarters of the Klan for Kemper county, were at the
grocery store of John W. Gully, at DeKalb. Here the

whisky was doled out which inspired their hearts to deeds of chivalry in masks. Here the Gullys and Dr. Fox, (says the evidence quoted,) when in solemn conclave, designated the men upon whom the visitations of their savage lust should fall, and the various detachments of the Klan throughout the county were there assigned their particular and especial duty. James Watts and A. G. Ellis, two sycophantic and hypocritical lawyers, were their legal advisers, when, at the same time, they were under pay of Judge Chisolm and his friends, for the transaction of legitimate business.

Thomas W. Adams, a white man, having been a clerk in the republican constitutional convention, which met in Jackson in the winter of 1868, had thus incurred the wrath of Fox and the Gullys, and accordingly was carried from his house at night and whipped. While undergoing the tortures of the lash, Adams was told by the Klan that their object was to teach him to take the whip like a "nigger," as he had been associated with the "niggers" in the "radical" convention. Adams knew and recognized many of the men engaged in this affair, gave their names to the military, and they fled the country.

Henry Greer, a negro, was dragged from his bed at night and severely beaten.

Near Tamola, in Kemper county, three negroes were taken out, the first one killed and his house burned down; the other two were carried to the woods near by and there murdered. One of the victims was a woman

Near the same place a colored school house was

burned immediately after the opening of free schools in the State.

At McLendon's another school house was burned, rebuilt and burned again.

In August, 1873, a colored school house, on the place of the widow Chisolm (Judge Chisolm's mother), was burned at night.

The same night Charles Robinson, a young man and teacher of a free white school, was staked to the ground by disguised men and threatened with death. His life was spared on condition that he would leave the county. It is needless to add, perhaps, that he left.

Also a negro named Peden was known to have been killed by the Ku Klux.

In the month of July, 1865, Thomas Burton waylaid and shot on the road, near Narkeeta, a colored woman and boy. Burton's apology for this crime was that they had been stealing watermelons. Not having been in any way interfered with for this dual murder, Burton soon after committed another, if possible more heinous and diabolical. He went to the cabin of an old negro living in the woods, fully two miles from any other inhabitant, and there shot and killed him, and then undertook to burn the cabin, to cover up the evidences of his guilt.

Miles Hampton, a colored man, living on the place of Mrs. Thomas Hampton, was shot in the night time, by Ku-Klux, and killed.

Below is a letter, written by Mrs. Chisolm to a friend. which affords a very clear and striking picture of the treatment herself and household received in those days at the hands of these chivalrous gentlemen. From its perusal alone the women of the country will learn something of the sacrifices which southern ladies are called upon to make whose husbands have sought to uphold their manhood in the free exercise of their opinions. The letter bears date DeKalb, June, 1874.

"The disturbing elements were for a long time busy with their intermeddling tongues, supposing Chisolm 'rode the elephant,' as the saying went; and finally it began to be whispered that the life of no man was safe who did. On going to his office one morning he found in his room, just under the door, an engraved card, I presume about three inches long and two wide. On this was printed a black coffin, and just below a skull and cross-bones; on the back were the letters 'K. K. K.' On his bringing it home I treated the whole thing as a joke. About the same time the negroes of the county were much alarmed by accounts of a wild man, who made steps 'seven miles long,' who had hair reaching to the earth, and lived in the swamps, and ate all the negroes that crossed the bridges. This *man* proved to be the Ku-Klux Klan. The name and story of the wild man, together with the bit of engraved card, afforded infinite merriment in our house for both myself and children, Mr. Chisolm having already understood its meaning, but refraining from explaining because of the uneasiness he knew it would give me This was in the year 1869 and '70. During that year there were regularly appointed club meetings held, with open doors,

by the republicans. The democracy have held their
meetings with locked doors. While Mr. Chisolm would
be at these meetings the creatures would come around
our house at night. We were then living out half a
mile from town, and on the hillside was a grove of
trimmed oaks. These they would get among and use
the most obscene and profane language, professing to
address Mr. Chisolm, knowing, by virtue of sight, that
he was in the court house. One night they shot into
the house, at the dog, which was lying on the steps;
but the gate was far from the house, and they were
afraid to come quite to the fence. I had no other
earthly protection than an old negro woman (Nellie). I
made her come with me and carry a gun; but before
I could fire it they ran out of sight, under the shadows
of the trees. Later Mr. Chisolm had started to Macon,
and they, finding it out, came at night and took about
twenty-five panels of fence down on each side of the
road, for the purpose of letting the cattle destroy his
crop. Some kind friend sent him word at Scooba,
before he left town. He hastily returned, and, going
among the friends of the Gullys, Hulls, Waddles, etc.,
said very publicly he would deceive them about being
absent, and the next time they approached his house he
would himself be among the trees, with several guns,
and would select his men to suit his own judgment, and
he would be sure to bring them down. This stopped
most effectually that manner of attack. Time passed
on, and Mr. C. had the attack of asthma I have told
you of in a previous letter, in which even the doctor

thought he had died. The news went to a county church. The gentlemanly Gully, with horrid oaths, asserted that he ought to have been dead long since. But God, for that time, disappointed him, and my husband began to recover, as if by magic. Tuesday night, after the severe spasmodic attack of asthma, (it occurred Sunday), he being still unable to lie down, heard the voices of men outside the gate, and, listening attentively, found they were in quite a large number. He told me what he thought; but not being able to stand, I took him his pistols. He then found his strength insufficient to hold and cap the pistols. I sat by him, and, with his directions, re-capped both his pistols and his gun. All this was right in front of the door, Mr. Chisolm being still unable, from his terrible attack and from his present difficulty in breathing, to go into another room, and not thinking best to close the door. It was also known his friends and kindred had been visiting him from his mother's neighborhood, and they could not know how many were still there. I called from the house for the negro man who lived nearest us, and who was in our employ. The Ku-Klux began, during the stir, to go away, starting in the direction of the Hulls. I had it afterwards from one who professed to be an eye-witness, that they ate supper at John Gully's that night, having their horses hid in the woods, where they also dressed in their hideous robes and masks. Soon after, another negro told one of our hirelings they took a meal they called breakfast at four o'clock in the morning at old Phil Gully's By nine o'clock of the next day Phil and Bob

Gully, of Neshoba, were at our house, Phil, in his great
affection, riding through the gate and seeming inordi-
nately glad to see my poor, persecuted husband. He
inquired if he saw any Ku-Klux the night before. Mr.
Chisolm told him he was not able to see out at anything; but heard men talking, and, being sick was not
in a state to be dragged about by them. Old Gully
then said he thought they would not hurt a sick man,
and announced himself opposed to any such plans.
But not yet done, he insisted, as soon as Mr. Chisolm
would be able to ride, I should put him in a buggy and
take him to *his* house to spend a week eating watermelons; to his house, in the very edge of the creek
swamp and the very nest of the Ku-Klux, where you
might blow a horn and bring up a small army."

From late in 1869 to 1871 — less than two years,—
some thirty-five negroes were known to have been killed
by the Ku-Klux; while whippings took place almost
nightly.

By the untiring perseverance and courage of Judge
Chisolm and a few of his associates, the military were
enabled to raid heavily and more successfully upon the
Klan, and numbers of them were arrested, while others
fled for safety and sought new fields of glory in more
hospitable climes. Many of the men apprehended, says
Judge Chisolm in his testimony, told by whom they had
been encouraged to perform these acts of lawlessness.
Foremost among the names given in this connection were
those of John W. Gully and Dr. Fox. Gully and Fox
had promised these young men to defend them in case

of arrest by the courts or military, but when adversity came they had failed to do so in a single instance. This had the effect to well nigh destroy the influence of the Klan as an organization, but the work of death and outlawry did not stop here.

CHAPTER V.

The patient reader is asked to follow still farther this dark pathway, strewn with the accumulated evidences of a generation of crime defiant and unwhipped of justice.

John McRea, who, as stated before, became Chisolm's successor in the office of probate judge, being a republican and a young man of brilliant promise, had also incurred the displeasure of John W. Gully; and, a rencountre between McRea and Hull, in which McRea chastised Hull severely with a cane, added to the intensity of Gully's hatred, and, as in the case of Chisolm, Rush and others, pursued him unrelentingly.

A brief account of McRea's life, and the manner of his death at the hands of John W. Gully, becomes necessary here, and will be of interest to the reader. The story is furnished by McRea's sister, now living in Kemper county. It is given in her own language:

"It has often been denied that politics had anything to do with the frequent killing of republicans in Kemper county, but I am certain it had in the case of Judge John McRea. It is true, there was a family feud between the McReas and Gullys that dated back to the fall of 1848, and as the Gullys bragged they never forgave, so did the McReas. They had been on speaking terms for years before the death of Judge McRea, but nothing more. The hate was still there, and was only fanned into a fiercer flame in the bosom of the Gullys by the sons of the McReas rising in life, and displaying talent which the Gullys never possessed. Judge McRea was a lawyer of ability. When the war broke out he went as a private soldier and rose to the rank of adjutant of his regiment. He remained in the army until the summer of 1864, when he came home and said his conscience would not permit of his continuing in a cause he abhorred. He was the first white person in Kemper to declare himself a republican, which was in the year 1867. John W. Gully was then sheriff, and from that time commenced to insult and persecute the Judge. McRea was appointed probate judge by General Ord, and afterward circuit judge by General Ames. McRea and Chisolm began to recommend men to office whom they knew had been loyal. This gave an additional offense to the Gullys, as they knew they would have to go out, for they had formerly controlled all the offices of the county. John Gully had a habit of blustering and scaring people out of his way. He tried it several times with Judge McRea, but found it would not work, and concluded he would use buckshot. In February, 1869, as Judge McRea was leaving the court house, in company with the district attorney and his (McRea's) father, an old gray-headed man, Gully came walking down the street, singing a vulgar song, evidently for the purpose of insulting Judge McRea. McRea stopped and told his father and the district attorney to stay there until he could 'see that man,' meaning Gully. Gully had his pistol in his hand, and Judge McRea had his in his sheath. As McRea advanced Gully backed, neither speaking a word, until Gully reached his own store door, when he reached out a double-barrel gun, dropping his pistol. McRea's father had followed, and was just behind the Judge. When Gully raised his gun, McRea said: 'You are not coming it right, sir;' when Gully fired. McRea kept advancing and Gully discharged the other barrel. Then McRea said: 'now I'll get you,' and rushed forward. Both barrels of Gully's gun took effect in McRea's face and breast. When Gully fired the last barrel he ran into his store and shut the door after him, and on through the store into the back room and shut that door. By the time McRea got to the door he was so blinded by blood that he could see nothing. He pushed the door open and fired every round of his pistol in the store, playing sad havoc with dry goods, but failing to hit Gully. The Judge sank down from loss of blood, and was taken up by his father and some negroes, carried home and a doctor sent for; but Gully's gun happened to be loaded with squirrel shot. Some boys had had it the day before and had drawn the buckshot out, and left it loaded with small shot. The doctor examined all the wounds, and when asked by McRea's brother-in-law, in the presence of McRea's sister, if any of the wounds would prove fatal, answered: 'No! unless some of the shot penetrated the lungs. In that case consumption would be likely to follow.' McRea was confined to his room three weeks, and when he left it, he had a cough which was pronounced consumption by the best physicians in the country. He died in the March following, 1860. As he was the first McRea who had ever died of consumption, as far back as the family could be traced, the world can judge what brought it on. The case was not brought before the grand jury of Kemper until after the death of McRea. Then there was no indictment found."

It was not far from this time that a man named White said some disagreeable things about Higgins, a school teacher. Higgins was a spirited fellow, and compelled White to give a written retraction or apology for the insult offered. Floyd, who was a brother-in-law of White, felt himself aggrieved that White should have been compelled to do an act so disgraceful as to publicly retract a statement he had once made and declared to be true; and accordingly headed a crowd of desperadoes, who went to Higgins and tried to force him to give up the writing which White had been induced to sign and deliver to him. White and his crowd, who resorted to every species of insult and threat, were unable to obtain the coveted paper. Higgins, feeling very much incensed at this attempt to bully and humble him, grew desperate, and on the following day met Floyd and killed him, never trying to escape nor in any way avoid the consequences. There still being no jail in DeKalb, he was sent to Macon, in an adjoining county, and there confined. When brought back for trial, Higgins was placed in charge of a man named W. G. Edwards, who was so well liked by the democracy as to have been made a constable by them. Higgin's father and Edwards, together, contrived the escape of the prisoner. They were all members of the same great and good party.

Some time after this Dennis Jones, a negro living on some railroad land near Judge Chisolm's plantation, procured the Judge's consent to build a fish trap in the creek which ran through it. One night, when on his trap, Dennis was shot and killed. His wife charged the crime upon a white family living near, who had accused Dennis of stealing their cotton.

Bob Dabbs then had a difficulty with a freedman named Walter Riley, and one night soon after, he was shot by some one from the outside of Gully's grocery, and mortally wounded. Before his death he expressed the belief that it was the negro with whom he had had the difficulty who shot him. This is all that is known at this time of the killing of Dabbs.

As late as the year 1875 Mr. Morton, while returning to his home in Kemper from a trip to Meridian, where he had been, as was thought, for the purpose of collecting a large amount of money, was waylaid and shot by some one in ambush. Two negroes were suspicioned, arrested by Judge Chisolm, while sheriff, convicted and sent to the penitentiary. Morton is still living.

In November, 1869, James L. Alcorn was made governor of the State by the popular vote. Soon after Alcorn's election Judge Chisolm was appointed sheriff, holding the office by virtue of the appointment until 1871, at which time he was elected by the people, and Charles Rosenbaum, a young man of sterling character, who was born and raised in DeKalb, was made his chief deputy.

In the canvass of 1871, John P. Gilmer, a native of

Heard county, Georgia, where he was born February 29, 1846, an ex-Confederate soldier, and a young man engaged in the mercantile business in Scooba, came out, openly declared himself a republican, and supported Judge Chisolm for sheriff. Up to this time Gilmer's character was good, and no slighting or slanderous word had ever been whispered against him. He moved in the first circles of the society where he lived, and the very worst that could be said of him was that he partook too much of the reckless habits of a very large majority of the best young men of the country. Being of good reputation otherwise, bold and vigorous, it is not to be wondered at that a sagacious man like Judge Chisolm should make the most of the acquisition of Gilmer to the ranks of his party. But alas! in the case of Gilmer, as in that of every white man who ever voted the republican ticket in the county, he was soon branded as the vilest of all vile men.

It was here that "Hal" Dawson first appeared upon the scene in Kemper county politics, and for a time he is made a central figure in the progress of this story. Dawson was said to have sprung from a family, that, for generations back, were noted chiefly for their deeds of violence; and Dawson, himself, was admitted by all to have been a very dangerous and desperate man, especially when under the influence of liquor. He appeared from day to day in the streets of Scooba, clad in a gaily colored flannel over-shirt, open at the neck, without vest or coat, and pants fastened at the waist with a large leather belt, from which was generally suspended a six-

shooter and a knife of enormous size. The grotesque-
ness of this costume was increased by the addition of a
pair of very high topped boots, and Mexican spurs the
size of a small cart-wheel. " Hal" was in the habit of
getting drunk every day, and his special province seemed
to be to curse and abuse " radicals." He had repeatedly
threatened Gilmer, and said that he would either drive
him from the town or kill him. On one occasion, while
Gilmer was sitting in front of his store, reading a paper,
Dawson leveled a gun at him from across the street, and,
with both barrels cocked, called the attention of the
by-standers to the fact that he was about to shoot the
paper out of Gilmer's hands. Some of his friends
insisted that he should not do it, fearing that Gilmer
himself might receive a portion of the lead. Dawson
insisted that he could hit the paper without injury to
Gilmer, and while the friend stood in the street, at a
distance of ten or twelve paces, with his feet some
twelve inches apart, arguing the case, in momentary
expectation of seeing Gilmer killed, Dawson fired
between his friend's legs, and killed a hog just in the act
of passing, a short distance behind him.

It was while in the enjoyment of one of these festive
occasions that Dawson was especially abusive of Gilmer,
and Davis, Gilmer's clerk, who was a member of the
board of registration. Taking his pistol in his hand,
Dawson went into Gilmer's store. Passing Gilmer at the
door, as he entered, he remarked that Davis was the man
he wanted to see. Davis had taken a position in the back
end of the building, armed with a double-barrel gun, which

he discharged at Dawson, just at the moment the latter fired his pistol. Dawson then wheeled around, facing Gilmer, who also fired, when Dawson fell to the floor mortally wounded, still grasping the pistol in his hand. On examination by Mr. Clay McCall and B. F. Rush, who went into the store upon the instant, it was found that one chamber of Dawson's pistol had just been discharged, and upon further inquiry the marks left by the bullet were discovered in the wall.

The killing of Dawson was at once heralded abroad as a most wicked and diabolical murder. Gilmer and Davis were both arrested and carried to DeKalb, the county seat, and there placed in charge of the sheriff. The prisoners were confined at the court house, in charge of an officer.

The night following the killing of Dawson, Gilmer's store was broken open by a mob, his goods taken out into the street and all not carried off were burned. The following day a crowd, numbering ten or twelve men, went from Scooba to DeKalb, and demanded of the sheriff that the prisoners should be carried back to Scooba for a preliminary hearing. To this demand the sheriff—Judge Chisolm—would not consent, knowing very well that if Gilmer and Davis ever passed from under his guardianship they would be shot in cold blood; besides, under the sheriff's watchful eye, and at the county seat, was the proper place for prisoners to be held charged with a high offense. An examination was had in DeKalb, at which three magistrates presided, one of whom, at least, was a democrat, and the prisoners were placed under a bond of $3,000 each, for their appearance at the ensuing term of the circuit court.

Dawson's rare genius in the indiscriminate use of the pistol and knife, had endeared him to a large circle of kindred spirits in Alabama, who determined to avenge his death. These Alabamians, from the inception of the Ku-Klux Klan in the South, seemed to take the lead in deeds of atrocity. They were more thoroughly organized and much better mounted and equipped than the brotherhood in almost any other portion of the South, and they seemed to take special delight, whenever an occasion presented, and "occasions" could be gotten up to order at any time, in setting an example before their weaker and less effective brethren along the Mississippi border. As a proof of their superior skill and entire willingness to make their benefactions general, let us turn aside for a moment and call to mind the riot and massacre at Meridian, which took place on the 6th of March, 1871, a few months prior to the occurrences just enumerated. From a recital of its lamentable details it will be seen how these organized desperadoes were in the habit of invading the soil of an adjoining State, committing there any act of violence and blood which their savage hearts might prompt them to do, and then to return with all the pomp and assurance of a conquering army.

CHAPTER VI.

Meridian, like Scooba, is situated only eighteen miles from the Alabama line, and thirty-five from DeKalb. Previous to the riot this place was one of the most thriving in the State, and indeed, it might be said, the whole South. It was a new town, having sprung up mainly after the close of the war. Its reputation for thrift and enterprise was becoming national, and men and money from every quarter of the union were fast coming in and adding to its wealth and prosperity. William Sturges, a native of Connecticut, and well connected in the place, a gentleman of culture and refinement, was first made an alderman and afterward appointed Mayor by the Governor. Sturges' private character was good, and his executive ability such as to have made for him an excellent reputation as Mayor. But unfortunately for him and the prosperity of Meridian, he was also a "radical," and had been "foisted upon the people" by the indirect aid of the poor and despised negro. Under Sturges' supervision the colored men were organized into clubs, had a band of music, and, when occasion required, they would promenade the streets, just the same as their white brethren do, and ever have done since the formation of the government. They were in the habit of holding public meetings, at which time the speeches made, it is true, were not always such as to please a democratic auditory. The marching of large bodies of negroes, headed by a band of music playing patriotic airs, in itself was sufficient to arouse a spirit of hostility toward the newly made citizens; but their "incendiary" speeches threatened the "peace and dignity" of the "good people" of the place. To use a phrase which has long since passed into a proverb, Meridian must be carried, "peaceably if we can, forcibly if we must."

Some time in the winter preceding the riot, a man named Daniel Price, who had been driven from his home in Alabama, took refuge in Meridian, where he became a teacher of a free school. Price had been a gallant soldier in the cause of the Confederacy, was a man of fair education, a native of the South, and, so far as has ever appeared, of good character. He was followed to Meridian by an armed band of his old persecutors, who sought his life. Price had drawn around him a number of friends, who secreted him from his pursuers, who returned after raiding the town in wanton violation of the law and the peace and dignity of the people. But a few days after this occurrence there arrived a negro from Alabama, who stated that he was a deputy sheriff; that he came with the proper papers to arrest certain parties in Meridian — colored men — and carry them back to Alabama. Never having shown his authority to any one, it was believed that he was an impostor and trying to act without the shadow of law; and one night, when prowling around among the negro cabins, some one assailed and gave him a severe beating, whereupon the negro returned to the persons who had sent him. This treatment of their agent in crime was made a pretext for a second raid into Meridian, by the same men, and this time they came in larger numbers and with an apparent determination to do greater mischief. Price, meantime, had been arrested, charged with having committed the assault upon the Alabama negro, who had falsely assumed to be a deputy sheriff. Price had given bond for appearance, and, on the day set for examination, about seventy-five or one hundred of these Sumpter county desperadoes came, as they said, to "see a fair trial." Price was urged by his political friends to leave, as it was believed by them that he would be murdered if he remained, and that a general riot might follow. He finally left, forfeiting his bond, which was paid by his republican associates, and he has never been seen or heard from in Meridian since. Their failure to reach Price seemed to increase the fury of the marauders, who took entire possession of the town, and especially the "groceries." Republicans, both black and white, were insulted, and the most prominent among them finally sought safety in flight. Unable to find a pretext for a general riot and killing, the mob, after kidnapping three negroes, returned with them to the place of their rendezvous, in Sumpter county, Alabama. What then was done with the negroes is not known to this day.

Saturday night of March 4th, but a few days, or weeks at most, from the date of these occurrences, a fire broke out in the storehouse of Sturges, Hurlbut and Company, in Meridian, a leading and influential mercantile firm, doing business in the place. Theodore Sturges, of the house just named, was a brother of William Sturges.

the mayor. The mayor was his brother's bookkeeper, and lived with him at his home. Notwithstanding this fact, absurd as the statement will readily appear, it was rumored that the fire had been set by some negroes, at the instance of William Sturges.

A whole block was burned down, and the house of Sturges, Hurlbut and Company was destroyed. During the progress of the conflagration riotous conduct on the part of a few prominent negroes was charged by the whites, and one colored man was knocked down with a gun and left for dead. Still unable to find sufficient cause for a riot, that night several negroes were arrested and carried before Judge Bramlett for trial the following Monday — March 6th — on a charge of "trying to incite riot," by making incendiary speeches, etc. A large crowd of white men, citizens of Meridian, had assembled, ostensibly to listen to the trial; but really, as will soon appear, for the purpose of raising a general row and killing off the leading republicans, black and white. A white man was placed upon the stand to testify against Warren Tyler, one of the accused. Tyler, who was an unusually bright and intelligent fellow, and brave as Julius Cæsar, proposed to impeach the testimony of the witness. The idea of a negro attempting to impeach a white gentleman's evidence was too much, and could not be endured. The witness seized a heavy walking stick and approached Tyler, who stepped backward to avoid a blow aimed at his head. Tyler had been disarmed when arrested, and exhibited no weapons, according to the testimony of a large number of witnesses; and it is admitted that when

he went into the court room he had no arms. But as
the man advanced with his stick a score or more of pistols were drawn by the whites, who began an indiscriminate firing. A pistol shot, coming from the side occupied by the whites, struck Judge Bramlett in the fore-
head, and he sank dead upon the judicial bench. Two
negroes were killed on the spot; one of them was
robbed and his throat cut from ear to ear. The court
room was cleared in an instant, and for three long days
and nights riot and murder ran wild and unbridled
throughout and far beyond the limits of the town.
Before ten o'clock at night of the same day one hundred
and fifty armed men arrived from Alabama, who were
immediately joined by the "good citizens" of Meridian.
Together they took possession of the town, and high-
ways, and railroad trains leading into it. Colored men
were hunted down like wild beasts, and shot in the fence
corners and in the woods, where many of them fled for
safety. Their churches and residences were burned, and
hundreds fled the country, never again to return.

That portion of the mob made up from Meridian was
composed of doctors, lawyers, ministers and merchants
— those who pray loudest in public places — and in short
the "better class" of people. The mayor took refuge in
the house of his brother, prepared himself with a dozen
loaded guns and pistols, and determined to sell his life
as dearly as possible. Several times the mob, three or
four hundred strong, surrounded the house and demanded that Sturges should be given up or the house
would be burned down over his head and those of the

brother and his family. Bar rooms were forced open, and whether willing to do so or not, their keepers were compelled to pour out whisky without stint or limit, and of course without price; and the natural brutality of the rioters was warmed into more active life by the aid of that most potent of all weapons in the hands of a Mississippi democrat—bad whisky. About twenty lives were sacrificed.

It will be remembered that Sturges was a good Mayor, and in the thorough and impartial discharge of every duty pertaining to his office, the very best the town has ever had, before or since. This fact, perhaps, was the cause of greater hostility toward him than anything else; for, in the matter of making arrests and in the treatment of all parties who came or were brought before him in his official capacity, he made no distinction on account of color or previous condition. But his integrity was so great, and his administration so thorough, that he had many friends and admirers, even among his worst political enemies; and, when it was found that his life was to be sacrificed, a few came to his assistance by the way of remonstrating with the mob, and promising that if his life was spared, he should leave the town and the State for all coming time. These terms were finally agreed upon, and under an escort of one hundred men, headed by R. L. Henderson, a brave man and a good citizen, he was taken to the train and permitted to depart.

At the time of the riot, Meridian had a vigorous and growing population, numbering nearly or quite six thousand. To-day about twenty-five hundred souls can be counted there, many of them without thrift or prosperity. Along the busy streets that were traversed, in those dark days, by this wild and ungovernable mob, with loud shouts and curses, brandishing in mid air the torch, fresh lighted in the burning ruins of the humble negro cabin, and carrying in their belts the knife or pistol dripping with his innocent blood, can now be seen whole blocks of solid brick whose only occupant is the cockroach, the bat and owl. " Democracy" has reigned there supreme from that day to this, but the hand of the assassin and the torch of the incendiary have neither of them been suppressed. There are no more bands of music in the hands of jubilant and happy negroes discoursing patriotic airs, it is true; the "good people" are spared all that, but arson and murder, bankruptcy and ruin meet the beholder on every hand.

Only last year the mayor of the city was indicted for and convicted of crime and misdemeanor while yet in office, and was subsequently re-elected and still holds that honorable position, with the decree of the court, unanswered, hanging over him.

CHAPTER VII.

The night of the 3d of November following the killing of Dawson, a body of Alabamians, numbering about fifty men, arrived at DeKalb, in Kemper county, and stopped at the grocery store of John W. Gully. For a week or more previous to this an unusual stir had been noticed among the leaders of the Klan in DeKalb. At Gully's, frequent and prolonged meetings or consultations had been held, by day and night, for some purpose, nobody knew what, save the plotters of iniquity themselves. This had aroused a suspicion on the part of the republicans in the place, that a "big job" of Ku-Kluxing was soon to take place somewhere in the county, and they were on the alert, and, upon hearing of the arrival of the Alabamians, Gilmer and Davis, who were still in custody, accompanied by one or two others, by consent of the sheriff, took to the woods for safety. Judge Chisolm, himself, had gone home that night, sick with asthma. No clearer statement of what followed can be given than that taken from his testimony before the investigating committee, at Washington, a few months later. This evidence will be found on page 250 of the official report of the committee. In answer to a question by Mr. Poland, the chairman, Judge Chisolm said:

"On the night of the 3d of November, I was not well; I am frequently bothered with asthma, and I did not go to sleep until three o'clock in the morning. About that time I got relief and slept soundly. About half an hour before sunrise of that morning, a colored boy came to my room and woke me up. He had been my driver since the war. This boy came into my room and told me that old Aunt Charlotte, who lives over on a hill near by, had told him that there was a body of armed men between my house and town, secreted in the bushes; that they had been there for two hours or more. I told the boy that I supposed it was only some men who had been drinking down there and had alarmed Aunt Charlotte. After looking to see what time of day it was, I turned to go to bed again. The colored boy started out, and when he got to the door, said: 'Judge, the old woman thinks she is positive about these men, and she is very much alarmed; had you better not see something about it?' Said I, 'Hezz, you go and see who they are; if you know nothing about them, and they are armed, come back and we will go after the rascals.' I then laid down and went to sleep again, and slept until after sunrise, when my little boy came in and told me that my breakfast was waiting for me. After eating, I started out in the direction of DeKalb, when I met the boy, in company with another from Neshoba county, whom I had under arrest. I had arrested him, but had released him to stay at my house until the Neshoba court met. I met them at the gate, and saw that this boy was very much excited. He said, 'Judge, there are twenty-five or thirty men over there after you.' Said I, 'What in the d—l are they after me for? Where are they?' He said, 'They have gone on in the direction of DeKalb.'

Said I to Hezz, 'you go by and tell Joe, Tom and April to get their guns and come up town as quick as they can.' I went back into the house, got my gun and went to the court house. I did not go, however, the regular way. When I got into town, the people were very much excited. In fact, before I got there, I had been told that several notes had been sent to my house warning me of the presence of these men. The notes did not reach me, as they were sent by the big road. I asked the people what it all meant, and they told me that they knew nothing about it. They had seen these men come into town and go in the direction of my house, but they had no idea where they were going, and thought it was a body of soldiers. They were on horses, and when they came back from my house they stopped at John Gully's grocery and got a gallon of whisky, and then left town. The first boy they seized— the one I had there from Neshoba county—said they arrested him about day-light, when going toward my house. He said they asked him what his name was and where he was going. He told them that he was going to the house of a man by the name of Judge Chisolm. They asked if I was the sheriff. He said he knew nothing about that; that he had never been in DeKalb until three days before; that a man had come up to Col. Powers' place, brought him down there and put him in jail, and that a man called Judge Chisolm came there and took him out of the jail, and told him to stay at his house until the court was held in Neoshoba county. They then asked the boy if I did not come that way in coming to DeKalb. He told them I did. He was asked if I could get to DeKalb by any other route, and he said not that he knew of. They asked what time I usually went to DeKalb, and the boy said, generally about sun-up. One of the crowd then struck him with a stick and said, 'G—d d—n you, you are playing off on us; you know he goes to town sometimes by this trail-way.' They proposed to hang him to make him tell; but a man they called 'Captain' interfered and said that the boy might be telling the truth; that he might have just come and might know nothing about what was there at all. When the other boy whom I sent from my house went out they were in the bushes, and he said that when he got within twenty steps of them, while not on the look-out, and before he saw or knew anything about them, they had up their guns and pointed in his direction, and told him to come to them, and of course he went. They asked his name and he told them. They then asked where I was, and he said I was sick. They asked if he did not live with me, and he said he did. They said, 'How is it that he is sick this morning, when he was not sick last evening?' The boy said he knew I was not sick the evening before, but that he had just left me in bed sick. They wanted to know if I was not going to DeKalb; he said he did not know anything about that; that he only knew I told him I was sick, and that he supposed I was not going to DeKalb that day. They were along the road that leads to my house. I lived at that time about a mile out of town. The men took him down to the other corner, to a crowd of men, and asked for a man they called 'Captain'—no other name—who was in the bushes, and said to him: 'There is a boy that lives with this fellow, the sheriff; he says he is sick.' The 'Captain' and this Lieutenant (the boy said they called him Lieutenant, he did not know his name) went off and talked a few minutes together. He heard one of them say, 'What will we do now?' The Lieutenant said to the Captain, 'Well, I am not going to the house.' The Captain said, ' Neither am I, by —— !'

They then called their men up and sat these boys down on a log, and ordered them not to tell one word of what had been said to them or they would kill them. One of the men took out a watch and gave the time of day, and told him to remain there one hour; said that they were going down to Saluda creek, below town, and were going to stay there until Saturday night, when they would come back. This is what they said to the colored boys; but they did not remain. I got up a posse of fifteen men, black and white, and followed them to the Alabama line, to Paineville, in Sumpter county."

Effort was made to indict Gilmer and Davis for the killing of Dawson; but so notorious was Dawson's character, and so generally was it known that he was the aggressor on the occasion in which he lost his life, that, notwithstanding the bitterness which existed against Gilmer and Davis on account of their politics the idea of a prosecution was abandoned.

The names of the grand jury before whom the facts

were brought are here given. Eight of this jury were democratic and seven were republican; and members of this jury assert that every possible effort was made to indict, but the evidence would not permit. Mr. B. Y. Ramsey, the attorney who represented the State before the jury, and a fierce democrat, instructed the foreman that the cases could not be separated; that if one was indicted the other must be. This the acting district attorney said in answer to a question as to whether or not a case of malicious mischief could be found against Gilmer, who, it was alleged, shot Dawson after he was dead. One of the witnesses called by the State — Mr. Scott Spencer, also a democrat — testified before the jury that he tried repeatedly on that day to prevent Dawson from going into Gilmer's store. The following are the names of the jury: J. A. Burton, Thomas W. Adams, Peter E. Spinks, William Dear, T. H. Morton, J. J. Tinsly, J. C. Carpenter, C. P. Chancey, George Robinson, Thos. Orr, Henry Greer, James Welch, Kinch Welch, Charles Nichols, and Henderson Ramsey.

CHAPTER VIII.

But the persecution of Judge Chisolm by the Alabamians whom he had so far thwarted in their endeavors to take his life, did not stop here. In another chapter it is stated that the family connections of Dawson had for generations been conspicuous for their deeds of violence and blood. Among these there was a man named Dillard, who lived at Gainesville, not far from the Mississippi line. Dillard had been somewhat conspicuous as a politician, and at one time claimed to be a republican; but in some way forfeited the confidence of the party, and failed to receive promotion correspondingly great with the estimate he had placed upon his own services and ability. From this Dillard returned to his first love, and again became a violent democrat.

To one unacquainted with the history of southern politics it is not readily understood how a man can one day espouse a principle, and as quickly turn and become its most bitter and uncompromising opponent. The case becomes very plain, however, when the fact is known that there never was any *principle* involved in the conversion. When Southern men once affiliate with the republican party and fail to reach the object for which the evolution is performed, they are forced to take the opposite extreme in going back, in order to be admitted to anything like equal terms of membership within the ranks of the party once deserted. They are like northern men living in the South during and since the war, who become the most violent and senseless advocates of the old doctrine of secession and State rights — a cause which, from education and instinct, most northern men abhor — becoming more bitter, violent and unreasonable in advocating the genuine southern faith than the most radical natives of that section. With all the assumed hostility to the teachings so early instilled into their hearts and minds, it is often difficult, and indeed many times impossible, for them to retain the confidence of the citizens among whom, at best, they can be but casually and incidentally adopted. This, however, is only applicable to those of either section who have reversed the old orthodox creed of " conviction before conversion." An honest conviction will often carry men far beyond the reach of selfish motives, even into the jaws of death itself, and so it is with the southern man who sacrifices social position, incurs the bitter and relentless enmity of kindred and early friends, and whom the tortures of the rack itself are unable to swerve from those principles of right and humanity which cannot be enjoyed within the ranks of the old party of disunion, hatred and intolerance.

In the early fall of 1874, more than two years after the killing of Dawson, when in Meridian, on his return from a trip to Jackson, Judge Chisolm was confronted by a large, " red-faced " man — to use his own language — in company with one or two others, all appearing to be intoxicated. At every turn he was met by these men, with an angry and insulting stare. The Judge purposely avoided them, dreading the consequences of a difficulty, which he believed to be the object of the strangers. The following day, as soon as the business hour of the morning arrived, Judge Chisolm repaired to the law office of Messrs. Hamm & Fewell, and while there, very much to his surprise and somewhat to his annoyance, who should come in but his disagreeable acquaintance of the day before. Preferring to transact business more privately, and still fearing a collision, the Judge, and one of his attorneys, stepped into an adjoining room, and not until then was he made aware of the fact that his "red-faced" friend of the day before, was none other than Judge Dillard of Gainesville, Alabama, the man who was known to have been foremost in inciting the invasion from Alabama into Kemper county, two years before, for the purpose of killing the leading republicans there. Judge Chisolm, soon after, went on the street in further pursuance of his business, and, when turning a corner, met an old acquaintance, who was at the time engaged in conversation with Judge Dillard. This friend, addressing Judge Chisolm, and not knowing that any enmity existed between the two men, proposed the usual courtesies of an introduction. Dillard at once very indignantly drew back, and said that he was not "receiving introductions to d—d radical scoundrels! You are a d—d, thieving, radical scoundrel, sir!" said he to Judge Chisolm. Still dreading the consequences of a difficulty, Chisolm, very much against his will, and sense of honor, again turned away and crossed the street.

Dillard, in a voice loud enough to have been heard half a square distant, continued to curse and abuse Judge

Chisolm in the grossest manner, heaping upon him every insulting epithet known to the vocabulary of a southern politician of the democratic school. From this man, Dillard, Judge Chisolm received insults far greater than he had ever before taken from any one when himself placed under the most adverse and unfavorable circumstances, and much less had he borne them from any person who stood singly and alone; and while Dillard still had him at a disadvantage, Chisolm resolved to die rather than tamely submit to farther abuse. Having on a heavy talma, he threw it back so as not to be incumbered in drawing his pistol, and then started across the street toward Dillard, who, seeing him coming, drew and leveled his pistol and warned Chisolm off, still cursing him. Judge Chisolm drew and steadily advanced, the eyes of each peering into those of the other, without saying a word. When two or three steps distant, both fired. The shot from Judge Chisolm's pistol struck Dillard in the side, when they clinched, Chisolm throwing his antagonist to the ground, and, holding Dillard's weapon with one hand, he was just in the act of shooting him with his own pistol which he held in the other, when a gentleman ran up and wrenched Chisolm's revolver from his grasp. Believing it was a life and death struggle, and not knowing how many men he might yet have to contend with, Judge Chisolm determined upon finishing this one, at least; and still holding Dillard prostrate, he reached into a hip pocket and drew another small pistol, which was quickly taken away from him, and the two were separated.

Before a warrant had been issued for his arrest, Judge Chisolm placed himself under the protection of the sheriff, Capt. Bob Mosely, and while at the house of that officer, to save his little daughter, Cornelia, then attending school in the place, unnecessary alarm, he sent her a note, stating that he had had a difficulty with Judge Dillard — whose designs upon her father's life the daughter knew very well — and that he had wounded Judge Dillard, but himself was unharmed. This statement did not satisfy Cornelia, who feared that if her father had escaped thus far, he would again be attacked by greater numbers and finally killed, and she at once hurried to his room. The writer remembers well the appearance of this girl as she came into the presence of her father that day, when, choked with sobs, she undertook to return thanks for the kindly offices of those who had come to the aid of her beloved guardian. Though many evidences of her fondness for him had been witnessed before, this left a deeper impression than all else. Little was it thought then, however, that her unselfish devotion and sublime character — afterward so strikingly displayed — would soon place her name upon that scroll which holds sacred in the hearts of all true men and women, the good and virtuous deeds of those gone before.

As usual, the cry of "an attempt to murder by an infamous radical" was raised. Judge Chisolm was arrested and placed under a bond, and at the following term of the circuit court, which convened very soon thereafter, a true bill was found, charging him with "assault with intent to kill." At the May term of the next succeeding court — in 1875 — he was tried on the indictment and acquitted; the jury returning a verdict in fifteen minutes, without consultation or disagreement. William M. Hancock was the presiding judge, who, although a republican at the time, had been considered good enough by the democracy to hold the same responsible position for many long years, and through succeeding terms of office.

In the year 1872 J. P. Gilmer was elected State senator to fill a vacancy occasioned by the death of Hon. W. S. Gambrel, a sketch of whose life and career as a union man and republican in Kemper county it now becomes necessary to present. The account given below is furnished by a lady, who for many years lived neighbor to Mr. Gambrel, and who knew the family and their circumstances well. The statement of this lady is also corroborated by a member of the family now living in the county. Neither the intelligence nor the integrity of this witness will be questioned by any one. Her own language is quoted as nearly as possible.

"At the opening of the war Mr. Gambrel was engaged in teaching school near a small town now known as Rio. He had the misfortune to have been born in Ohio, but came South in early youth. He married into a southern family, and was at the opening of the war, the father of several children. Always a strong unionist, and so expressing himself, he did not vote on the matter of secession, because there was no other ticket out. Soon after the opening of hostilities his wife, then in delicate health, became insane. His task was a hard one. The 'committee,' as usual, while staying home from the war themselves, 'waited on him' and ordered him out. He refused to comply, and soon after some of his pupils were taken sick. They accordingly decided to hang him if he did not go to the war, pretending that he had poisoned the spring because his pupils were southern children. Mr. Gambrel told them that his wife and children, his home and interests were all southern. Judge Chisolm, by his firmness and courage, prevented the hanging. Senator Gambrel was then compelled to leave his afflicted wife and little ones to the mercy of the savages of Kemper. He went into the army and delivered himself a prisoner in the first engagement, without firing a gun. The Federal officer gave him a position, the writer is quite sure, in the commissary department. He lived frugally, and at the war's ending had saved money enough to bring home many much needed comforts. His poor wife had recovered her mind, but the family were in squalid poverty. He soon placed them in comparative comfort; but the trials Mrs. Gambrel had passed through sent her speedily to the grave. He was often compelled to leave his children under the protection of the colored cook. One night Mr. Gambrel returned and retired without awakening his family. Before morning a negro broke into the room occupied by some of the older children. A faithful old servant gave the alarm, and when the father came in told him who she *believed* the intruder to be, and showed the place and manner of his escape. Mr. Gambrel afterward confronted the supposed guilty negro — Flander

Jones—and struck him a blow in the face. Jones then went to the cabin of another colored man, and, while there, ran some bullets, which he told were for the purpose of killing Gambrel. When the two met again a collision took place in which both fired pistols. Jones' shot took effect, from which Mr. Gambrel died soon after. While on his death-bed he was visited by Judge Chisolm and many other friends."

Mr. Gambrel often spoke, when in the presence of the lady who furnished the above facts, in the highest terms of Judge Chisolm and his many acts of friendship, at a time when he, being a republican, had no other friend. After reconstruction and the organization of the Ku-Klux, Gambrel became the object of their especial hatred. His house being visited on several occasions, he was finally compelled to call in his neighbors —a few who were friendly and whom he could trust— to guard himself and premises at night.

But it is now told by the great party of reform that Gambrel was killed at the instance of Judge Chisolm, to make room for Gilmer in the State senate.

CHAPTER IX.

In November, 1873, Judge Chisolm was again elected sheriff by the popular vote, his term of office expiring in 1875, at which time the political destinies of the whole State passed into the hands of the "good people." The registration of the vote of the county, since 1868, shows the numerical strength of the blacks as compared with that of the whites, to have been very nearly equal. There never was but a slight preponderance of one over the other; yet for the constitutional convention of that year there was a republican majority of six hundred and eighty-seven votes. For Governor Alcorn, in 1869, there was a plurality of over two hundred; and in 1871, at which time Judge Chisolm was first elected sheriff, the excess of votes for his ticket reached about one hundred and eighty. In 1872 it was over four hundred, and at the State election for governor, in 1873, the republican majorities for the various offices reached as high as two hundred. From these figures it will be seen that the strength of the party against which this terrible hostility existed did not depend upon the newly enfranchised citizens. From the very outset it must have received a large native white vote; for upon no other hypothesis can these large majorities be accounted for.

During the terms of Judge Chisolm's office he accumulated property, as every other sheriff in the State did, without a solitary exception. But the duties pertaining to that position meantime were performed by him to the letter, and he was never accused of misappropriating a single dollar of public funds, notwithstanding the continued hostility of those who sought his destruction in every possible way.

That Judge Chisolm sometimes resorted to extraordinary measures to carry out the object in view will not be denied, and that the circumstances justified such means will hardly be doubted. A verification of the old adage or proverb of "fighting the devil with fire" would have been warranted, no doubt.

Owing to the unsettled condition of the whole State and the inauguration of free schools in the county, the building of bridges and other changes and improvements made necessary by the results of the war, taxation became heavy, though credit had steadily improved; and, as already stated, county warrants had advanced since the accession of the men then in power, from twenty-five to seventy-five cents on the dollar. The greatest tax imposed upon the county, and the one of which the people complained most, was that made necessary by the establishment of the free schools, and it is a fact worthy of notice in passing, that the board of school directors for the county were, during the whole time, pronounced and uncompromising democrats, as they were also "racy of the soil."

It is a fact, well known in the South, that for several years immediately following the close of the war, and even before that period, "speculations" in cotton became very common. In these operations vast fortunes were sometimes made, and almost every one, who, by dint of good luck, or what often proved better, a determination to "win," could in any way become a party to a "cotton transaction," entered upon it with a will equaled only by their cupidity. To this good day it is the pride and delight of these men to relate their experience in running off "the great staple" and swindling the government out of its dues; and, what is more to their shame, "Uncle Sam" was not always the sufferer. In these transactions John W. Gully was a fortunate adventurer. His operations began early, and while he was sheriff a large amount of money placed in his hands by the Confederate authorities, with which to buy cotton, was thus expended, but when the war closed he sold the cotton then on hand and put the money received for it in his own pocket. This cotton, by the terms of the surrender, belonged to the United States government, and should have been so accounted for. Several hundred bales were thus appropriated by Gully. This fact is well known to the people of Kemper to-day, and Gully himself often boasted of his shrewdness in thus swindling the "d—d Yankee government."

Having learned from experience the best manner of conducting little schemes like this, who so well as Gully could plan an illicit operation of the kind, place an enemy in the foreground, and make him appear to one unacquainted with the "ways that are dark," as the principal operator and beneficiary? It was not, however, until the year 1871, when Judge Chisolm became a candidate before the people for the office of sheriff, that an accusation, in the form of a "cotton speculation," was brought against him. It was then charged by John W. Gully, that Chisolm, in the capacity of probate judge — some four or five years before — had forged an affidavit by which a number of bales of cotton, supposed to belong to the United States authorities, were placed in the hands of gentlemen who clandestinely disposed of them, as Gully had disposed of that which fell into his hands. This charge Judge Chisolm refuted at the time it was brought, and despite the efforts of his unscrupulous enemies, was elected sheriff by a large popular vote. In the fall of 1876, when he became a candidate for Congress, the same old story was renewed. It was done after the Judge had left his home and gone into the canvass, beyond the reach of friends who were conversant with the facts, and through whom he might be able to establish his innocence, and first appeared in the Jackson *Clarion*, a leading newspaper of the State. To this publication Judge Chisolm replied on the first opportunity, through the columns of the same paper. As will be seen, his letter was written while at Greenwood, one hundred and fifty miles distant from home.

CARD FROM W. W. CHISOLM.

GREENWOOD, MISS., Oct. 16, 1876.

Editors Clarion: I respectfully request that you publish this, my reply to certain charges which appeared against me in the columns of your issue of the 3d inst., and ask that other papers which have copied the article will likewise do me the justice to copy this. If there are those who think I have been slow in giving attention to

this matter, I will state that, as a candidate for Congress,
. I have been busy in the canvass, away from home, and
have been compelled to rely upon a correspondent to
procure such documentary evidence as I deemed important for my vindication.

Your readers will remember that the main charge, and
the one upon which all the others are based, was contained in the affidavit of one George L. Welsh, and
which I here reproduce:

THE FORGED AFFIDAVIT.

(Perry Moore was dead when this affidavit was made.)
THE STATE OF MISSISSIPPI, }
    Kemper County.   }

Before me, W. W. Chisolm, judge of probate in and
for said county, personally came Perry Moore, to me
well known as a just and reliable citizen in said
county, who, after being by me duly sworn according to law, deposeth and says, that he was with the
United States forces under the command of General
Sherman, in the county of Lauderdale, in the year (1864)
eighteen hundred and sixty-four, in said State of Mississippi, on or about the 20th day of February, of said
year, on the road leading from Marion Station to Hills-
boro, in Scott county, Mississippi, and he, the aforesaid,
saw at one White's gin, on said road, about eight or ten
miles from Marion Station, the said United States forces
put fire to and burn one hundred and eighty-four bales
of lint cotton (184), belonging to Robert J. Mosely.
They, the United States forces, stated and told me it
was by order of General Sherman.

                            PERRY MOORE.

Sworn to and subscribed before me, this, the 2d day of
[L. S] February A. D. 1867.
            W. W. CHISOLM, Probate Judge.

THE FRAUD ACKNOWLEDGED.

I certify that the foregoing is a true copy of the original papers, and that the name subscribed thereto, purporting to be the genuine signature of Perry Moore, is a base forgery, and so admitted to me by W. W. Chisolm, at the time I arrested said papers in his hands. Said Chisolm was at that time Judge of the Probate Court of Kemper county, and I was Clerk of said court.

GEO. L. WELSH.

DEKALB, MISS., September 30, 1876.

To convict this poor wretch, Welsh, of being at once a simpleton as well as a liar, I call the attention of the public to the following extract from the records of the Probate Court of Kemper county:

STATE OF MISSISSIPPI, }
   Kemper County. }

To the Honorable John McRea, Judge of the Probate Court of said county:

The undersigned, Jordan Moore, petitions your Honor to grant him letters of administration on the estate of Perry Moore, deceased, of said county, and in making this petition would state that said decedent departed this life on or about the *eighth day* of February, 1867; that he died without a will, seized of effects in said county, upon which it is necessary that administration should be had, and in duty bound your petitioners will ever pray. JORDAN MOORE.

Sworn to and subscribed before me August 12, 1867.

GEO. L. WELSH.

THE STATE OF MISSISSIPPI, }
   Kemper County. }

I, H. Rush, Clerk of the Chancery Court, in and for said county, do hereby certify that the foregoing is a correct copy of the letters of administration upon the estate of Perry Moore, deceased, as appears upon file and on record in my office at DeKalb, this October 23d, 1876.   H. RUSH, Clerk.

Welsh says that Perry Moore was dead *before* the affidavit in regard to the cotton was made, and that was on the 2d day of February, 1867; and yet Jordan Moore made affidavit, before this same George L. Welsh, that Perry Moore died on or about the 8th day of February, 1867. See how plain a tale will put a lying scoundrel down. By the records of his own court he stands a convicted liar. Need I say more? I would not trouble myself to say this much to people who know this Welsh; but many read the *Clarion* who have no means of knowing what reliance is to be placed in this fellow George L. Welsh. So I present them these two papers, that they may have no difficulty in determining.

Now, upon this slandrous charge of Welsh, all the superstructure of persecution against me has been raised. Proving the foundation to be false, what becomes of the edifice?

This same George L. Welsh says that "he arrested Perry Moore's affidavit in my hands; that I admitted that it was a forgery; that he demanded my resignation, and I did resign." I congratulate Welsh in doing what he seldom does — stumbling upon one scrap of truth; for "I did resign." But that I did it upon the demand of George L. Welsh, or any one else, is a falsehood too infamous to be coined by any other than his brain, notoriously fruitful in such productions. When I resigned my successor was appointed upon my recommendation. Where we are both known, the idea of George L. Welsh *demanding* anything at my hands will sound preposterous indeed. Alone and together he would not risk his carcass within reach of the toe of my boot, except he was acting the part of a cringing cur.

Affidavits from Thos. H. Woods, District Attorney, and Jas. Haughley and Wm. B. Lockett, members of the grand jury in 1868, declare that I was indicted for forgery in uttering the Perry Moore affidavit. That may be true; but I was present at the close of that inquisition, and never heard of it. If so, it was *ex parte*, and founded, doubtless, upon the testimony of Geo. L. Welsh, who we see has written, and doubtless then swore, that Perry Moore was dead before the affidavit was made. Whatever the grand jury thought, if they ever found such a bill upon Welsh's testimony, it is now beyond dispute that he lied, and lied in the face of his own records. It is true that the records of the court were stolen in 1868, and that a Ku-Klux cap was found in the office after the thieves had departed.

But, whether I was indicted or not, the fact remains that fourteen terms of the circuit court had been held in Kemper county since that time, and I have never been called to answer.

In addition to this, I may say that this is not the first time this matter has been before the public. In 1871, an anonymous letter, addressed to Governor Alcorn, appeared in the *Clarion*, containing substantially the same charge. It was a subject of investigation by the Governor, but he became satisfied that it was a malicious slander, and subsequently appointed me to the office of sheriff of the county, to which position I have been twice elected, since that time, by the people who knew of Welsh's slanderous falsehoods, and knew what value to give them. It is true that I was expelled from the Masonic lodge. Welsh is a Mason, so were his coadjutors. Pending the movement against me in the lodge, I was assured by T. C. Murphy, S. Gully and Charles Bell, that if I would be quiet politically, it would be all right in the lodge. Having been taught, even before I became an entered apprentice, that the obligations of

Freemasonry would not interfere with my religious or political opinions, or duty to my God, my neighbor and myself, I declined to yield to the demands of the "brethren," and was expelled because I was a republican, and forced to avow my sentiments.

Besides showing how basely slanderous and false this creature Welsh is, I might introduce him in a new act, and cast another shadow upon his character, by showing his connection with county warrants in Kemper county, and other deeds, darker still. But at present I am only engaged in proving him a liar, too distinct and unequivocal for the public to regard. I may give a chapter on other elements of his character hereafter, if any one should question his business.

Very respectfully yours, etc.
W. W. CHISOLM.

As appears, fourteen terms of the circuit court passed, and although there is no bar to the statute in certain criminal cases, in which "forgery" is named as one, the indictment was never renewed, and for a very good reason, no doubt: The one originally found had failed in accomplishing the villainous work for which it was procured, and a further waste of time was deemed inadvisable. Thus vanished the second and only specific charge of dishonesty ever brought against Judge Chisolm while living.

But we pass now to an account of treachery scarcely equalled in the annals of crime, and certainly an atrocity evincing a degree of recklessness and disregard of law never before attained in a community claiming to be governed by the dictates of common humanity.

In the month of October, 1874. some one, in the night-time, entered the room of a daughter of George Calvert, who lives in the southwest Beat of Kemper county. The young lady awoke, in great alarm, and just in time as she believed, to see some one, whom she did not recognize, run through the door and escape before the family were aroused. Suspicion of this grave offense centered upon one of two negroes living on the place, but no evidence whatever, and no circumstance tending to strengthen this suspicion, was ever obtained, farther than the boy was not found at home that night; his own explanation of his absence was that he had been out, as he had often done before, to witness a fox hunt in which some gentlemen were engaged not far away. Notwithstanding this he was taken into custody, without process of warrant, or any legal arrest, and carried to DeKalb, when the deputy sheriff, Charlie Rosenbaum, very properly refused to take the prisoner, save only in the manner and form prescribed by law.

It was believed by the leaders of this affray that an opportunity was now presented for carrying out a long cherished desire: that of murdering Judge Chisolm, and making it appear as the voluntary act of the whole community. The arrest of the negro was on Saturday, and all that night and the next day — Sunday — couriers were riding to every part of the county, and even to adjoining counties, in hot haste, with a lying report on their tongues to the effect that the negroes, headed by Judge Chisolm, had risen in great numbers and were then marching on the poor and defenseless whites, killing, burning and ravishing as they went; though it never appeared where this march began, nor in which direction its desolating pathway led. Yet the "good people" were quick to credit any story of the kind, and, by the following Monday, at least five hundred armed and mounted men, ready for any act of villainy which, in their barbarity, might seem to be necessary for the "public safety," had assembled in the neighborhood of one J. L. Spinks, a justice of the peace. To further whet their appetites for blood, and encourage the doubting and timid ones, the negro boy was taken out amid the shouts and yells of the savage throng, and hanged to the limb of a tree. But, as Judge Chisolm was all the time at his home in DeKalb, following his legitimate business, as the negroes were also at work in the cotton fields throughout the county, this Quixotic war upon an invisible foe must be turned to account in the manner and form originally designed. The killing of one poor negro, on a campaign of such gigantic proportions, was a very unsatisfactory result, and the real object of the "race war," as this affair was styled in Kemper county, soon began to develop itself, and in the following manner:

After consultation among the leaders it was determined to send a note to Judge Chisolm, asking him to come out and aid the "good people" in suppressing the riot and bloodshed likely to take place, as he was well known to all parties, was the executive officer of the county, and had more influence than anybody else. Accordingly the note which is copied below, was sent to him by the hands of the following named gentlemen, as appears by the envelope in which it was addressed:

"A. McMahan, J. E. Driver and others." From this it would seem they were calculating on "driving" a good business. The writing is all in Adam Calvert's well known hand. The paper itself emanates from a lodge of peaceful and unoffending grangers. Here it is:

MOUNT PLEASANT GRANGE,
No. 230.

J. R. DAVIS, Master.   J. L. SPINKS, Sec'y.

"MOSCOW, MISS., Oct. 1st, 1874.

"JUDGE W. W. CHISOLM, DeKalb, Miss.:

"*Dear Sir:* We have been requested by at least some two hundred persons now assembled at J. L. Spinks', Esq., to inform you that we are proud of the conversation you had with Archey McMahan and A. P. Davis in regard to the excitement now in our Beat about the negroes rising in arms against the whites. We have additional evidence to substantiate our fears upon. We have arrested several negroes, and the proof is positive against them. We do not intend to do anything in violation of the law or anything without reflection. We intend to defend ourselves in case the negroes come upon us, as they say they intend to do. We insist on your immediate presence at J. L. Spinks', Esq., to-day, just as soon as you can possibly come. We assure you that you will be treated as a gentleman, and hope you will not fail to come.

"Respectfully, your friends,
"ADAM CALVERT,
"J. L. SPINKS,
"JOHN R. DAVIS."

The names affixed to the above are those of old and responsible citizens. Two of them at the time were peace officers. With this message McMahan and Driver were at once dispatched to Judge Chisolm, at DeKalb. The fact of the communication being sent to him at all is in itself a proof of the hollowness of the pretense under which this mass of rioters had come together. They knew very well, before a single step had been taken, that Judge Chisolm was at his home; that himself and the colored men of the county were as free from the thought of instigating riot and bloodshed as a sleeping infant. But believing their appeal to have been made in good faith, Judge Chisolm was about to ride out to the place designated, in answer to it. His friends, more cautious than himself, thinking a scheme was on foot to take his life, besought him not to go, and he was finally prevailed upon to heed the timely advice. Thus the object of the conspiracy was thwarted, and this "race war," began for the purpose of shedding innocent blood, failed ignominiously, save only in the hanging of one poor negro.

The admonition of friends saved Judge Chisolm's life on this occasion, as that which follows will clearly prove. David Calvert — a brother of Adam Calvert — who married a sister of Judge Chisolm, afterward told his wife's family that he was cognizant of the note being carried to his brother-in-law on the occasion of the " negro hanging," near the house of Justice Spinks; that he knew the object for which it was delivered, and, to thwart the purpose of the men who sent it, and prevent the shedding of innocent blood, he himself dispatched a man with a message to warn Judge Chisolm of the danger which awaited his arrival at the scene of the riot. With no further evidence than the statement of an individual to prove a conspiracy like this, there might be found room for que oning its existence; but, fortunately, whatever evidence may be needed to dispel every doubt in the matter, is at hand, and will be found in the letter which follows :

RIO, MISS., September ——.

JUDGE W. W. CHISOLM :

Sir: I believe there is a plan on foot to assassinate you. This belief is founded upon an assertion that I heard one William Pearse make, in the presence of four respectable ladies. He said that you would be taken out of DeKalb before next Saturday night and meet with the same fate that the negro did who was hung on last Saturday near here. Other remarks, similar to this, have been repeated to me by your friends, which I will not take time to mention now.

There was an armed force of from fifty to one hundred men met at the grave of the hanged negro on Monday, to prevent the holding of an inquest.

Your friends in this neighborhood think you would do well to be on your guard.

My light is dim, and I don't see well at night.

I will close by saying that I hope you will be on your guard.

The hanging of the negro was an outrage of the blackest character. Your friend, as ever,

S. S. WINDHAM.

P. S. The excitement in the neighborhood is great.

The above was written and sent to Judge Chisolm by a special messenger. Mr. Windham, its author, was an honest and kind-hearted man, although a democrat and a brother-in-law of Adam Calvert. His opportunities for knowing the facts were the very best, and his statement in writing, over his own signature, will hardly be doubted.

The fact that he is now dead and out of the way of all harm, accounts for his name being given here.

CHAPTER X.

Amid all the disparaging influences by which he had been surrounded; violently assailed in person and in character; hunted at night by armed bands of ruffians; when leaving his home on business, compelled to go under cover of darkness by one route, and return secretly by another; branded and pointed at as one in every way mean and despicable, Judge Chisolm had around him an intelligent and refined family, consisting of wife and four children. Cornelia, the oldest, whose name is now a household word, at this date had been some two years at school in Meridian, a bright and joyous girl, beloved and admired by all who knew her. After Cornelia came Clay, and then Johnny, whose memory is closely linked with that of his beloved sister; and Willie, the youngest. Their home at DeKalb was a model of taste without, and bore the unmistakable evidences of culture within; and what is better still, it was an asylum for the poor, without regard to color or political affiliation. Born and reared as children were under the ban of social ostracism, their society had been formed largely within the home circle. The want of social and friendly intercourse with the outside world seemed to have molded and endeared the family to each other. That unfailing perception usually accorded to woman had early enabled Cornelia to mark the expression of care and deep concern which, from year to year, settled upon her father's face as the result of the daily life of hazard which he led, and she had thus been drawn to him by sympathy as well as love; and this two-fold force, acting upon her naturally warm and impulsive heart, made her fondness for him fall but little short of devotion. Nowhere on the broad earth could there be found a domestic picture more pleasing than that presented around the hearthstone of the Chisolm's at DeKalb. As the Judge grew in power and influence, his charities were dispensed with a lavish hand, and these were not confined to his party friends. His generosity developed with his means, and, shocking as it is to humanity, scores of the hands which for years had taken food from his board, on that fatal and dark Sabbath were raised against himself and lovely children, and were among the first to strike them foully to the earth.

But for the present a casual glimpse of this picture must suffice. We have yet a long way to follow the unbroken chain of circumstances woven around the doomed man and his party adherents, gathering strength with the growth of years, and culminating at last in a crime not equalled even in the dark days of the reign of the bloody Robespierre, and ending with as complete an overthrow of every principle of law and right as ever marked the passage of that bloody era in the history of unhappy France. The story of the political contest of 1875 in Mississippi has never been told. The acts of tyranny and savage cruelty, the false swearing and utter disregard and desecration of the most sacred mandates of God and man, as yet are only recorded in the hearts

and memories of those who were made to suffer most;
and its horrors will not be recalled here, excepting so far
as they may have direct bearing upon the persons and
objects discussed in these pages.

Guided by the firm hand and unconquerable will of
one man, the county of Kemper, for a succession of years,
had stood the tide of hatred engendered by secession
and nursed by the overthrow of the " Divine Institution"
and the final elevation of the late slave to citizenship
and equal rights under the law, and that stronghold of
"radicalism" became an object of special attention by
the white-line democracy all over the State.   If the programme of intimidation, fraud and violence which had
been decided upon in their State councils could be made
to win in Kemper, then the first rays of the morning sun
of the day following the election in November of 1875
would fall upon a State "redeemed."   To this end the
barbed shafts of the best orators of the State were
turned upon this republican Thermopylæ, while the
native bulldozers were untiring and persistent in their
watchfulness and zeal.

A few weeks preceding the election the "great and
gifted" Lamar delivered an address at Aberdeen, which
the Vicksburg *Herald,* a leading democratic paper, commented upon as follows: "At Aberdeen, last Saturday,
Colonel Lamar made an eloquent speech. A better
democratic speech we do not care to listen to; and in
manly and ringing tones he declared that the contest
involved 'the supremacy of the unconquered and unconquerable Saxon race.' We were glad to hear this bold

and manly avowal, and it was greeted with deafening plaudits. We have never seen men more terribly in earnest, and the democratic white-line speech made to them by Colonel Lamar aroused them to white heat." * * * * * In another place the same paper makes use of the following language, which is calculated to serve well in connection with "Lamar's great speech:" "The wanton killing of a few poor negroes is something unworthy of our people. If the killing of anybody is necessary, we repeat what we have heretofore said: 'Let the poor negro pass, and let the white scoundrels who have fired his heart with evil passions be the only sufferers.'" The utterances above quoted were repeated, *verbatim*, by Lamar at Scooba, in Kemper county, a few days after; the only difference being that stronger language was used in that immediate connection, and the name of Judge Chisolm given as being the only man within the county whose power and influence stood in the way of the realization of their cherished hopes; and the people of Kemper were enjoined by this great statesman to carry the county, "peacefully if they could, forcibly if they must!"

The Saturday before the election took place, Prof. Thomas S. Gathright, for many years one of the most influential and popular educators of the youth of the State, made a speech at DeKalb, within sight of Judge Chisolm's house, in which he used words very nearly as follows. After repeating Judge Chisolm's name, he said: "Gentlemen, if you ever expect to have peace and harmony in your county, you must get rid of this man. I will not undertake to tell you *how* to get rid of him; that you know as well as I, *but you must get rid of him!"* Then, encircling his neck with a gesture, he raised his hand up and down several times in imitation of dangling some object from the end of a rope. This speech and pantomime were responded to with loud and continued cheers.

On the following Monday the same language was repeated at Moscow, a cross-roads store, ten miles distant from DeKalb.

The fact that hundreds of such harangues were made all over the State, pointing out individuals, and republicans indiscriminately, by local politicians and lawyers, lank, lean and hungry as most of them were, without character or responsibility, signified but little. But when such poisonous words fell upon the ears of an ignorant populace, direct from the lips of men like Gathright and Lamar, terrible consequences might be expected to follow. The natural result of this teaching upon a systematically organized body of men, sufficient in numbers when backed by the moral support of a whole people, to carry out and enforce whatever edict or dogma might take possession of their wicked hearts, was seen all over the State during that memorable canvass, but in no part was its influence felt more keenly than in Kemper county. To clearly illustrate its effects the testimony of John P. Gilmer, before the investigating committee, is given. On page 497 of the official report will be found the following:

"John P. Gilmer, sworn and examined by Mr. Teller."

"*Question.*—Where do you reside?"

"*Answer.*—I reside in Scooba, Kemper county, Mississippi."

"*Question.*—How long have you resided in Mississippi?"

Answer.—I went in December, 1868, to Scooba, and I have since lived there and at DeKalb. I was born in Georgia, raised in Alabama and have been in Mississippi since 1868. Have only lived in these three States. I was a Confederate soldier, and was in the political campaign of 1875 in Mississippi; was in several counties during the time. I then represented the district that my county is in, in the State Senate. I was a candidate for re-election. There are three counties in the district— Noxubee, Neshoba and Kemper. I canvassed Kemper county only; did not engage in the campaign when it was opened. At the time the republicans held their convention I was in St. Louis. They nominated their candidates for representative and county officers, but, for some reason, did not make any nomination for State Senator, and held a convention for that purpose after I returned. I had decided not to be a candidate for re-election. However, after being nominated, I concluded to go into the campaign. It was then about half completed. I made several speeches at Scooba, Wahalak, DeKalb and two or three other places. So far as the campaign was conducted, on both sides, there was considerable feeling. Large numbers of democrats attended the republican meetings, which was something unusual for them, and the speakers were generally interrupted with questions in various ways. So far as my individual recollection is concerned I do not think I was ever interrupted at all, on the stand, while attempting to make a speech. At some places reports would come to us that we could not have meetings; that we were going to be interfered with during the time of speaking; but the real excitement that amounted to anything seemed to be about the latter days of the campaign; that is, when I was present, at Scooba, Wahalak and DeKalb. We closed the campaign with public speaking, at Scooba, the Saturday before the election, which was held on Tuesday.

By Mr. Money.

Question.—"On Saturday?"

Answer.—"On Friday or Saturday; I will not be positive about the date. There was a gentleman up there, and I do not remember his name, from Enterprise. He had succeeded in getting a large portion of the colored element, and a great many white people, who were in there, and he was making a very bitter, and as I thought, a very incendiary speech. There had been threats made to me prior to that, in Scooba, by leading men, in this way: 'Next Tuesday, or the first Tuesday in November, your sort will go up, and you will have no longer any influence in Kemper county;' and even in terms worse than that, but I did not pay much attention to it. As there seemed to be some excitement that day, I went into the office of the mayor, Mr. Wood. There were present myself, Judge Chisolm, Mr. Miller and Mr. Duke. These threats had been made to me prior to that. They said: 'You shall not, as you have done heretofore, put the tickets into the hands of the negro and make him vote your way.' We were there consulting about the manner in which the election should be held. Judge Chisolm and I made the proposition to Messrs. Duke, Miller, Jones, and Wood, the mayor of the town, that we never had been guilty of these charges, and we had never forced anybody to vote any way except according to his own conscience, and we were perfectly willing to let it be understood by both sides that the democrats could electioneer as much as they pleased; but we would put tickets in some place where it could be understood that republican tickets could be had; and all parties who wanted to go and get a ticket, whether republican or democrat, could get them, and nobody should interfere with or talk to them at all, but just let them go about and vote as they pleased; and that on the day of the election we would have no canvassing whatever, and not try to influence a single vote. Mr. Wood was disposed to agree to that, but Mr. Duke would not. They were democrats. Mr. Duke said he proposed to canvass as much as he pleased. Mr. Jones said he did not intend that there should be tickets taken away from the negroes, and they cursed for having voted the democratic ticket, as had been done before — or as I had done, rather. I said, 'Mr. Jones, if you say I ever cursed any one or forced any body to vote any way but according to their own conscience, it is not so!' He said, 'That is the report all over the county.' I said 'That the report all over the county then, is a d—d lie, and the author of it is a liar!' At that time Mr.

Dunlap, the marshal, came in and said there was great excitement out on the street, and he wanted the police force of the town increased. Then I left and came around to the rear end of the store that myself and brother were occupying, and we got some goods boxes and assembled a big crowd and had some three or four speeches. While the speakers were interrupted occasionally, I did not see any excitement at the time; but during that evening and the Sunday following there were colored men who came to me, and some white men, too, democrats, and told me, in a confidential way, that they did not want their names exposed, lest it should result in their injury; but that efforts would be made to assassinate myself and Judge Chisolm, the leading republicans, on the day of the election; that Alabamians would be over there, and that on Monday night they would have torchlight processions, and that they intended to assassinate us. Mr. Orr, one of the managers of the election, told me: 'There is no use in talking! I am afraid to hold the election.'"

"*Question.*—Was he a democrat or a republican?"

"*Answer.*—He was a republican. Mr. Orr was a white man. He sent word to my room, late on Sunday night, that he had just been up to see his sister—whose husband was a democrat—near Wahalak station, that day; that she had sent for him to be sure to come there; that it was very important that he should go there. His sister had informed him that she had heard, from her democratic friends, what would be done with himself and other leading republicans there, and advised

him not to remain in Scooba, but to leave until after the
election, and have nothing to do with it. He seemed
very much alarmed. I knew there were good grounds
for being alarmed, but I did not know it was so bad. I
informed him that I did not think there would be much
trouble; that nobody would bother him; that these
reports might be put out for the purpose of scaring
him. That night there were couriers coming in from the
country and telling me of threats they had heard, and
asking if we could not get assistance in the way of
United States troops. They said that night-riders had
shot into the houses of the colored people, and there
were men traveling over the country at all hours of the
night. On Saturday and even Friday night previous to
this, I saw men coming in with guns. On Monday
morning these men were in the streets. There was a
crowd, and appeared to be great excitement. As I
walked down the street to my store, I heard curses of
'—— —— the radical party,' and '—— —— the
United States government,' and threats that, 'We ought
to hang them, —— —— them,' to a great extent all
along the streets. They were all white men and democrats, whom I heard make these threats. I had been
sent for by a personal friend, who was a democrat, and he
informed me that my life would be in danger, and that
in a very short time there would be a lot of Alabamians
over there, armed, coming for the purpose of assassina-
ting me; that, perhaps, they would go on to DeKalb and
assassinate Judge Chisolm and other leading republicans. I left for DeKalb; was advised by this friend to

go there, and take a by-way, and not the main road. I
started, knowing the country pretty well, and took trails
winding about a way I did not think was traveled
very often, except by deer and other wild animals of the
forest. I saw at the roads, as I would approach them
at the forks, that there were guards stationed, and men on
horse-back with guns. I got to the house of a man
living some six or seven miles from DeKalb, who I did
not think had much interest in politics. I had befriended
him on occasions, and I thought he would be a friend of
mine. I called for some water, intending to talk with
him. Said he, 'Gilmer, what is all this excitement for?'
I said, 'I do not know, I am nearly famished for water,
I do not see any men about.' I wanted him to tell me
if there was any trouble, first. He said, 'yes, there is a
young man who just left here, and several parties have
passed my house with guns. Young Mr. Overstreet
just left here; he came for my gun, and I refused to let
him have it. He said the negroes were fighting in
DeKalb, and that Judge Chisolm was at the head of it,
and the people were hurrying on to Sucarnochee bridge,'
a crossing about two miles from DeKalb, and he said to
me, 'Gilmer, if you go there, you will be killed.' I
replied that I guessed not. He said, 'I will just swear
that you will be killed; but don't say a word that I told
you.' I said, 'I want to get to DeKalb; can I get there
without going the road?' He says, 'yes, but there are
guards along the road every mile, and you cannot go in
that way to DeKalb without being assassinated.' I
said, 'You do not think they would shoot me down

without giving me some showing, do you?' He said,
'yes, I do not think they would say a single word to
you. That is the programme; not to open their mouths
at all, but just shoot you and Chisolm on sight.' I said,
'Well, then I should like to get you to pilot me through
the woods.' He said, ' I will go and show you about a
quarter or half a mile, and after that will show you a
road in which you will be safe.' We started, and when
about a quarter of a mile he got scared, seemed to be
very much excited, and wanted to go back and get his
gun. I waited for him. He told me that I had better
leave my horse and take through the woods by myself.
He went back, got his gun, and then said, 'I will go
with you a quarter of a mile further, and perhaps you
can make your way all right.' I insisted upon his going
with me, and finally gave him fifty dollars to go. This
gentleman conducted me some four or five miles through
the woods to within about two or three miles of DeKalb.
After crossing the creek I came upon a colored man and
his wife picking cotton; I did not know them, but they
knew me. The gentleman who piloted me absolutely
refused to go any farther. I asked the colored man to
go with me; he consented, and piloted me through
the woods to the town. Not very long afterwards his
wife told me that I had scarcely got out of sight when
two parties rode up, with double-barrel guns, inquiring
if I had passed that way; they said I was somewhere
in the woods trying to make my way to DeKalb. I
took the precaution, before leaving, to tell her if any one
came and inquired for me to say that I had not been

there, and she says that she so answered. I got into DeKalb and found considerable excitement there; did not go down the streets, but was nearly there when I met some of my friends, and found that a lying report had been put out about me. I had recently been to Jackson, and found that the story had been started that I had shipped arms to Shuqualak and to Scooba by rail, and, in addition, that I had brought a trunk from Jackson, heavily laden, supposed to contain amunition; also, that a wagon-load of arms had gone through the country to DeKalb from Jackson, for the purpose of arming the negroes, and, beside, we had shipped about forty barrels of whisky, which they claimed to be an unusual amount for that little town, and it was for the purpose of making the negroes drunk before attacking the whites. I was informed of this by republican friends. I asked for the informant, and they referred me to Capt. James Watts and E. G. Ellis, both lawyers and democrats. My friends said they had obtained their information from Watts and Ellis, and that the latter were talking about moving their families out of town to get them away from any trouble which might arise on account of a riot gotten up by the radical party. I asked Watts and Ellis if they believed any such thing. They answered that they did not think such a thing of me before, but that this report came from a very reliable source. My understanding was, they told me that Mr. Duke wrote the letter giving them the information. There was no truth in the report about the arms. If I had shipped those guns at either place, by freight or express, or sent a package, the agents at each of those depots were democrats and white men, and they would have known it. There was no excuse for the story and no truth in it. I would not have gone to the woods if it had not been for safety. Before going there was some excitement about holding the election. Mr. Brittain, Mr. Welsh, Dr. Fox, Mr. Ellis and myself, and some republicans, were in the conversation. These first were democrats. They told me that if the election was held at Scooba, the managers would not be interfered with. I told them that if they would write to their leading men to give these parties protection, I would write such a letter to Mr. Orr, one of the republican managers. I wrote the letter and then went into the woods. We staid there—Judge Chisolm, Mr. Rosenbaum, Mr. Hopper, myself and two or three others—for several days. We returned, either the first or second morning after the election, to our private residences, and did not go down town. I do not think there were more than three or four republican votes cast at DeKalb, a precinct which constituted a whole board of supervisors; and the colored majority there was at least a hundred, and perhaps more. Many whites vote the republican ticket when they can, and the democrats voted about the usual number."

This testimony is fully corroborated by that of Judge Chisolm, taken before the Boutwell Committee, in Jackson, but a few months before.

The campaign of 1875 resulted in the complete overthrow of every principle of republicanism in the State, and republican officials whose term of office had not expired, were unrelentingly pursued; for it seemed to be a part of the plan to drive them from citizenship as well as place. Governor Ames himself was finally compelled to yield to the edicts of a white-line legislature as radical, proscriptive and tyranical in the exercise of its power as the most unwarranted dictations of the Paris Commune. By his forced resignation, the democratic president of the senate *pro tempore*—J. M. Stone—became governor.

But the excitement and high blood which had been aroused in this revolution was not allowed to cool before the canvass of 1876 was begun. This, as in the case of the preceding year, is not made use of only so far as its history has direct influence upon the subject under consideration.

In the fall of 1876 members of congress from the various districts were to be elected, and while republicans had no hope of success, candidates for that office were put in the field, so that it could not be said they had meanly submitted without a second trial, and Judge Chisolm received the nomination of the party for the district in which he lived.

In June of this year Cornelia Chisolm, at the age of eighteen, graduated with the highest honors of her class in the East Mississippi Female College, situated at Meridian. In music and art she was especially proficient, having received the very highest plaudits in these branches which the institution and an admiring public could bestow. But the training received at school did not go far in making up the real worth of her accomplishments. Possessed of intelligence and judgment beyond her years, no opportunity for the acquirement of useful knowledge was allowed to go unimproved, and her mind was thus stored with a fund of practical information seldom attained by one of her years, no matter what advantages of wealth and position they may have had. Upon all the topics of the day, especially that of politics, in which her father took such a deep interest, and in the advocacy of which she knew his life had been so many times involved, she always manifested a concern equal to the importance of the subject, and few men or women, either in private or public life, are better informed upon those national questions which for the past ten years have agitated the public mind, than was this young girl.

Thus fitted for a useful and happy life, and full of hope for the future, she returned to DeKalb, where, in the Chisolm household and the hearts of the few associates found in the neighborhood, she was at once coronated queen of love and beauty.

CHAPTER XI.

Owing to violence and repeated threats of violence, there was no organized effort on the part of republicans to carry the county of Kemper in 1876; and this is true of a large majority of counties in the State.

The very atmosphere was filled with a spirit of hostility toward the national administration and the friends of republicanism everywhere, so perceptible and even appalling in its nature as to terrify the oldest and stanchest members of the party, and the men who had always been found in the front rank, themselves and their families ostracised and struck from the pale of good society — so called; branded and pointed at as felons and penitentiary convicts; assaulted, wounded and maimed; men of character, resolute and brave; in most cases in the canvass of that year failed to come forward and attempt an organization of the party, however slight and imperfect, and but little effort outside of the executive committee at Jackson was ever made to carry the State; while the colored voters slunk back into their cabins, voiceless and breathless, only too glad to evade, by such a course, the visits of midnight raiders, in black masks, armed with guns and whips. So effectual had been the reign of terror established over them that it was a common remark, whenever an opportunity presented for expressing themselves to a white friend and sympathizer, that, in the days of slavery their moneyed value was an assurance of protection to life, at least; but under the existing state of affairs that safeguard had been withdrawn, and there remained absolutely no guarantee whatever of life or liberty. Hence in Kemper, as in other counties, there were no clubs formed, and no meetings, of any kind, in the interest of republicanism were held. There was but one speech made in the county by members of that party during the whole canvass. Sometime in July, before the campaign had fairly opened in Mississippi, and before Judge Chisolm had become a candidate for Congress, while on a casual visit to Scooba, he was invited by the democracy there to make a speech, indulging the fond hope, as is believed their leaders did, that he would now abandon the cause of republicanism, then on the eve of entire dissolution, and become a bulwark of strength in building up the party of "home rule." But in the dark days of its adversity, as in the years of its prosperity, Judge Chisolm stood like a great rock, true to his principles and colors. His speech in Scooba that day was orthodox to the core; but he was listened to respectfully throughout. This act of courtesy seems to have been performed for a purpose, as subsequent events will show. Some two weeks following this without his knowledge or consent, Judge Chisolm was advertised, by means of posters put up in public places, to hold a "joint discussion," at Scooba, on a day set, with some orator named. Believing, from the treatment before received, that a spirit of fair play had seized upon the democratic heart and conscience, the Judge reluctantly consented. Immediately upon his arrival in Scooba he was quietly informed by friends that the feeling against him was bitter, and if he undertook to speak his life wonld be endangered. It is well understood by all who knew Judge Chisolm that he was not a man to be frightened with a shadow. If there was danger he must test and know the fact. Accordingly, the condition of an equal division of time was faithfully agreed upon. At the Judge's solicitation a large number of colored men were kept together for hours while three or four democratic orators harangued them. After the fiery eloqence of the democracy had ceased to burn, Judge Chisolm got up and quietly intimated that inasmuch as he had been invited there to "take part in a joint discussion," he should now be permitted to speak. Just at this time the gentleman in front of whose store the crowd had been standing, was impressed with the melancholy fact that the passage-way to his door was obstructed, and in consequence no more speaking could be allowed at that stand. But removing to a place near by, the Judge undertook the hazardous part which he was to bear in the "joint discussion." As predicted, he had spoken but a few minutes when he was interrupted, in a most violent and threatening manner, and curses, loud and deep, were heaped upon his head from every quarter. His life was threatened, and pistols were drawn to carry the threat into execution. After repeated efforts to quiet the mob, he was compelled to quit the stand in order to save his life.

Thus the campaign opened. But we will not attempt

to follow Judge Chisolm through all the devious windings of that eventful canvass. Its history, like that of the preceding year, is yet to be written.

As the election drew near, Judge Chisolm's appointments brought him closer to DeKalb. The last before reaching home was on the 3d of November, at Scooba, to which place it was understood he would go from Macon by rail, and a large crowd had assembled to receive him. Before leaving Macon, however, he had been urged not to go; if he did, it was said, he would certainly be mobbed and probably killed; that the "reformers," in force, maddened with bad whisky, headed by a band of desperadoes from Alabama, were in waiting for him, and nothing short of his blood would appease their appetites. Heeding the timely warning, the contemplated visit to Scooba was abandoned, and Judge Chisolm went across the country, that day, to DeKalb. Whether he acted wisely in so doing or not, is best shown by the conduct of the mob in Scooba when the train arrived on which it was hoped and believed he would come. Filled to excess with the democratic "elixir of life," armed with guns and pistols, bloated and red-eyed, with yells and imprecations which might shame the most hardened denizens of the regions of the damned, they rushed in a body to the station to "welcome" the expected speaker. The disappointment at not seeing him only increased their fury and hate. As soon as it was known that Judge Chisolm had gone overland to DeKalb, where he was advertised to speak on the following day, the mob, with increased numbers, at once set out for that place, taking with them a cannon, shot-guns, pistols and plenty of liquor, and all other equipments necessary to the safe and sure conduct of a campaign on the "Mississippi plan."

Arriving in DeKalb, that night, they moved stealthily to within fifteen paces of Judge Chisolm's door, just as his children were in the act of going to bed. The first warning the family had of the approach or intent of this band of outlaws, was the discharge of the cannon, which shook the glass from the windows of the house, and this was followed by the discharge of small arms, accompanied by continued beating of drums and yells of besotted men, who repeatedly called upon Judge Chisolm and the ladies of his household, to "get up and listen to the music," demanding that they should acknowledge the compliment of the serenade. These acts of barbarism were kept up around Judge Chisolm's home until two o'clock in the morning, and before noon of the same day the assault was renewed in a much more violent and threatening manner. Quite early, loaded shot-guns were carried into the jail building immediately in front of the Judge's premises, ready for use by the mob at any time, while the crowd, which had already assembled in large force, carried small arms which were frequently brandished and discharged in the air. About nine o'clock a note was handed Judge Chisolm by A. G. Vincent, over the signature of John W. Gully, "chairman of the democratic executive committee of the county," inviting the Judge to take part in another "joint discussion." He replied that the meeting, if one was held, was his own; that it was so advertised, and democrats had no right whatever to a division of time. He stated, further, that he believed it to be exceedingly dangerous for him to leave his house, and much more so to undertake a republican speech in DeKalb that day, as information had already reached him from the streets, that his life had been openly threatened. Mr. Vincent, although a fierce democrat, had the fairness to acknowledge to Judge Chisolm, afterward, that he acted wisely in refusing to accept this challenge. By this time the "citizens" had assembled to the number of three hundred or more; many of them uniformed with red shirts. Beating of drums, shooting and yelling was now the order of the day. The name of Chisolm was mingled with their curses and cries of "hang the —— radical scoundrel!" were heard by his wife and children at home. All day long, on that memorable fourth of November, was kept up a scene of drunkenness, debauch and riot which baffles description. A prisoner from the county jail named Spencer—being a good democrat— charged with waylaying and shooting in cold blood a young man just married, and at the time riding by the side of his young wife, was released from confinement and gave *eclat* to the festivities by joining the mob and shouting lustily for "Tilden and reform!" Repeatedly throughout the day, did this crowd of ruffians and jail-birds march by Judge Chisolm's door, to the tune of "Dixie" and the "Bonnie Blue Flag," firing cannon at intervals and pistols by volleys. The latter were at first discharged upward, but as the crowd became emboldened from the excessive use of liquor, and meeting with no resistance, the shooting was directed over the house and finally against it, when two or three shots were embedded in the pillars and weather-boarding. These chivalrous gentlemen, who could thus surround, menace and assault a house occupied by women and children, breathing in their faces the fumes of the pot-house, and hurling upon their heads obscene and blasphemous oaths, were headed by no greater man than Colonel S. M. Meek, of Columbus, one of " Mississippi's favorite sons.' A Chevalier Bayard; a man who must hide beneath the black cloth and clean linen that he wears a cowardly and craven heart. Close by the side of this *beau ideal* of southern chivalry, walked John W. Gully, the presiding genius of the demoniac festival.

For the purpose of throwing additional light upon this subject, a letter written by Cornelia Chisolm but a few days after these occurrences, is here appended. Little did this brave girl, whose sensitive heart then bleeding afresh from the wounds just inflicted upon herself and other members of the family, by the insults of a brutal and mendacious mob, think that this communication would ever find its way into a work of this kind, thereby adding a strong link to the chain of evidence showing the outrages practiced upon her beloved father during the progress of the canvass of that year. Its candor, frankness and depth of feeling—written to a private individual, and as it must have been for no other purpose than that of giving temporary relief to an over-burdened heart—give it the weight of a whole volume of testimony derived from any other source. Here is the letter:

DeKALB, November 13th, 1876.

My very dear friend :

In your kind letter, which came this evening, the contents of which I know are from the depths of your dear, loving heart, you ask me to tell you "all" concerning the late terrible assault upon our house by a band of drunken and riotous men. Now my dear ——, I am going to relate, as nearly as I can, the details of at least a part of the wrongs and indignities which our family have endured, and which wounded me much deeper, being aimed, as they were, at the one who is dearer to me than almost all else on earth beside—my darling father. These repeated insults to papa and his household came from the fact that he chose to be guided in his political acts by that which, in his heart of hearts and own good judgment, he deemed to be right—loyalty to his country and its flag.

Pardon me if I speak too strongly, and remember what has driven me to this. When papa received the nomination for Congress in his district we entreated him not to accept it, as defeat was certain, under the present administration of the laws of the State, which allows mobs of armed men to force the voters from the ballot-box and drive them from their homes; and, what is much worse, we knew his life would be in jeopardy every hour. Notwithstanding our appeals he accepted the nomination, and said he was determined to canvass the district, as he deemed it his duty to do. He had large audiences everywhere he went, and not only invited but insisted on his opponent meeting him at all his appointments and arrange for a joint discussion. Mr. Money—the opposing candidate—met him at only one place, and he forgot that decency required of him at least civil treatment toward a stranger, but instead procured the services of a band of music, and a large crowd of men, in battle array, uniformed with red shirts, armed with guns, swords and pistols, to heap insult after insult upon papa. When papa got up to speak two men were stationed on the stand behind him, displaying dirk knives and pistols. Papa then gave his opinion of such proceedings, and told them that he would not speak unless the stand was moved against the house, and all bullies put in front, where he could watch them, giving as a reason that he did not want to be stabbed in the back. They did as he requested; but when he began they commenced screaming and hallooing so loud that no one could hear him, and he was finally compelled to quit the stand.

A committee then came to insist that he continue his speech. He reluctantly consented; but had no sooner started again than they repeated their interruptions.

It was just the same everywhere he went. In Macon he was obliged to divide time with a democratic negro — Younger — in order to be allowed to speak at all. He had a good many friends there; but at most of the places he had no acquaintances even. He was to speak an hour and a half at Macon and the negro the same length of time; then papa to have half an hour in which to rejoin. Two of papa's friends overheard the democrats talking among themselves, and found that their plan was to kill him when he undertook to reply. These friends sent papa a note to that effect while he was on the stand, and he left just before the negro finished speaking. Another one of their committees went to his room to urge him to reply, but he sent them word that he would have no more to say.

In Shuqualak he did not speak at all, because he received intelligence convincing him, beyond any question, that if he undertook to do so he would be shot down from the stand.

He had an appointment at Scooba, but didn't even go there; for his friends, and enemies also, said that he would no sooner get off the train at that place than he would be shot by a crowd of Alabamians, who had come there for the purpose, at the instance of the editor of that vulgar and indecent paper, published in your place, the Meridian *Mercury.*

But now comes the "tug." The wretches hired the Gainesville band to come here, only to insult our family. On Friday night, just as we were all undressed for bed, and some of the family had already lain down, they marched up to our gate with a great crowd, "serenading," as they said, and nearly frightened me to death. You see I was then only just being initiated; others of our family had often seen the like when I was away at school. They brought the old cannon right in front of the door, and I devoutly prayed that it might burst and blow them all into the "fiery furnace," where I am certain they will eventually land.

Well, they left after finding how little they had accomplished; got some more men and whisky and came back about twelve o'clock at night and tried it over again. But all the family had to console and comfort me. I tell you I thought I should die. I hardly slept one bit all night. By the next morning at daylight papa's friends came in from all parts of the county, including four gentlemen from Macon. They were all at our house — about fifteen good, true white republicans, who swore they would die by their leader and best friend.

There were hundreds of negroes in town, and nothing but papa's constant and vigilant efforts kept them from firing upon the bloodthirsty demons as they passed by

on their march. They had the democratic flag, the band
— playing "Dixie" and the "Bonnie Blue Flag"—a few
ragged, old negroes and hundreds of villainous white
scoundrels, half of whom were owing papa for the clothes
that covered their backs. He stood on the steps and
cursed them in language more forcible that elegant. The
first time they yelled and screamed like the savages they
were, and one man shot off a pistol in the air. The
next time two or three fired, and a few more each time they
passed, until the shooting became incessant, and several
shots struck the wall, just by the door. At this time
nearly all the gentlemen who had been with us were
over at Mr. Gilmer's and Captain Rush's, to get Mrs.
Gilmer and her baby, and Mrs. Rush and her daughter,
to come to our house, as all of them had been insulted
and frightened nearly to death, while their men folks
were with us.

Several of the gentlemen were worn out, or crippled,
in the canvass, and so you see papa and brother were
about the only ones who could shoot to do any good,
and but for mamma's entreaties, they would have made
some of the beggarly dogs bite the dust.

I kept close to papa's side all day, and when he told
me that, if another shot was fired, he intended to kill
some of them, he begged me to leave him, because those
who did not run would fire at him, and he feared some
of the shots might hit me. I told him that I prayed
the same shot which killed him might also lay my lifeless body by his side. My dear ——, I once thought
that I never would tire of life; but, if such is to be mine,
death, if I could share it with my dear ones, would indeed
be a sweet relief.

Colonel Meek and John Gully headed the procession.
At one time Meek passed by with his arms around the
neck of a ragged, filthy and degraded negro. I call him
" degraded " not because of his black skin, but rather for

being found in such company, exchanging embraces with so low and disgusting a being as Meek that day proved himself to be. Next to Meek and the negro came "Bill" Preston. I shudder at the thought of desecrating these pages with the name—a young gentleman (?) of your town.

I have now given you some of the details of the insults we have received. When I see you I will say more, and, like the Queen of Sheba, who came to visit Solomon, you will exclaim: "The half has not been told me!" Again begging your pardon for having spoken, as I fear, too bitterly, but asking you to consider what we have all endured, with much love, I remain your friend,

NELIE.

The following is the sworn testimony of Judge Chisolm touching this same matter. It will be found on page 755 of the congressional report of last winter:

"*Question.*— Did you have any further meeting?"

"*Answer.*—Yes, sir; I had a meeting advertised at Scooba. Rosenbaum went home the night before and wrote me that I had better not come there, and advised me to go through the country to my home; believing, as he said, there would be a crowd of Alabamians there, and that it would be dangerous for me to go to Scooba. I took a carriage and went through the country to DeKalb. I arrived Friday evening, about half an hour before sun-down. That night, about ten o'clock, there came a crowd of men right in front of my gate. I suppose they were within twenty paces of the house; they had with them a band of music from Gainesville, Alabama, and they played and shot off their cannon and small arms, cursed, and asked me to 'come out.' My appointment to speak in DeKalb was on the following day. That is where I live. They returned about one o'clock that night, and went through the same demonstrations. The next morning there came in a good many of my white friends of the county — there is a right smart white republican vote there — a good many wanting to see me, and I not being down town, they came up to my house. It was tolerably early — I suppose ten o'clock — when I got a communication from Swanzy, and from J. W. Gully and some others whose names I forget. They signed themselves, 'by authority of the democratic executive committee.' I received this from the hands of a man named A. G. Vincent. I read it and said, 'Mr. Vincent do you think that I would be allowed to make a speech here to-day?' He said he did not think I would; or, perhaps, I could; I don't remember just what his answer was. I continued, 'I understand from a hundred sources that they will not let me speak, and I won't answer this note.' He asked me, 'why?' Said I, 'this carries a lie on its face. It sets out by stating it is a democratic meeting, when you know that such is not the fact; it is a republican meeting; the democratic meeting was held yesterday — that is, by appointment.' He said he had forgotten about that, and says I, 'I will not attempt to speak unless I am satisfied there will be no interruption. I am not afraid, under ordinary circumstances, of anybody interfering with me, but when you have got a crowd of two or three hundred men, I am afraid of what they may do.'

He went off and I did not see him again. A few

minutes after the crowd came around my house with their cannon and band. They did not shoot when they came the first time until they had passed the gate; but they cursed me very extravagantly. When they had passed they fired a volley of small arms, it seemed to me, in the air over the house. They went around by the grocery and took on some more whisky, I suppose, and then came back and fired all along by the side of my house, cursing me terribly, and saying, 'Come out! What are you in your hole for?' About the fourth or fifth time they fired into my house, and the bullets were imbedded in the walls. Since that time I have had a conversation with the same man who brought me the message—Mr. Vincent. He says that my proposition was right; he did not think I would have been permitted to speak, and said there was a strong probability I would have been murdered. I made no effort to speak. This was Saturday before the election. It was held on Tuesday. I did not go out of my house at all on that day, nor the day of the election."

CHAPTER XII.

By these "little acts of pleasantry," as this long list of outrages was styled by the virtuous citizens of Kemper and the press of the State, the complete overthrow of republicanism was secured, the organization of the party broken up, their newspapers suppressed, and in Kemper, as elsewhere, it was proclaimed and circulated abroad that a peaceful, quiet and impartial canvass and election had been held. But the perpetrators of these villainies in Kemper were not to escape thus easily. Some thirty or more of the gang which had wantonly assailed Judge Chisolm and his family were reported to the United States grand jury, comprised of men of both political parties, and indicted under that clause of the Enforcement Act which guarantees to every citizen who may be a candidate for office a full, free and uninterrupted canvass. Judge Chisolm, Gilmer and Hopper, in answer to a summons from the court, gave testimony before this jury.

Two or three unsuccessful attempts to make arrests under the finding of the court, by as many different deputy marshals, were made before process could be served on any of the persons indicted. Walter Davis, one of these deputies, was shot at by parties in ambush, while passing from DeKalb to Scooba, but escaped without injury. Papers were finally served, but there never was anything like a formal arrest made. The rioters took their own time for going before a United States Commissioner and entering into a bond for appearance at the following term of the United States Court. All this on the part of the authorities was characterized by the press of the State as the "most inhuman and uncalled-for act of tyranny and oppression ever perpetrated upon a free people."

It was sought by the Gullys, who had been foremost in every broil and iniquity perpetrated during the canvass, and some of whom were among the first apprehended, to clothe the arrests with all the horrors of an inquisition by the general government. Through their especial mouthpiece—the Kemper *Herald*—the democracy of the county was invoked to "rally to the defense of its outraged citizens." The Hon. Mr. Money, who had been the opposing candidate to Judge Chisolm in the canvass for congressional honors, having a high appreciation of the services rendered him by his constituency of Kemper county, responded promptly to their call, and addressed a letter to the *Herald*, which elicited the following editorial remarks :

"We received a letter a few days since from Hon. H. D. Money, in which he made arrangements to pay us twenty dollars for the purpose of defraying the expenses of our Kemper 'bulldozers,' and stated that he would pay more if it was needed. He expressed the kindest feeling of sympathy for those of his fellow-citizens of Kemper who were indicted, and declared his willingness and determination to bear his full share of all the result."

Thus it is seen that the conspiracy to intimidate and

murder was not confined within the narrow limits of a single county, nor were the poor "white trash" to do the bloody business and at the same time furnish the means with which to defray current expenses. The "fortunes" as well as the "sacred honor" of the leading men of the whole State were pledged to this work, and it was the moral and material aid lent by them that carried it into successful execution.

On the first day of January, 1877, following the arrests, a "citizens' meeting" was called at DeKalb, to give expression, in some substantial way, to the public indignation. It is not believed, as one might suppose, that this call was for the purpose of organized resistance to the Federal authorities. There was an object ahead, far more significant, and one which might be realized with less trouble and expense to themselves. It was the determination of the leaders then to assemble a large crowd of ruffians at DeKalb and take the life of Judge Chisolm and all his associates; for by so doing they hoped to destroy the last chance for a successful prosecution of their clan in the United States court.

The first of January came; but owing to a heavy fall of snow the night before—an unusual occurrence for that climate—and the bad condition of the roads, the "meeting" was not well attended. Besides, Judge Chisolm, knowing their intent, had quietly called around him on that day a sufficient number of his friends to guard against the possibility of an attempt being made upon his life. Ten men like Chisolm, when prepared, were able at all times to hold the "citizens" to a careful consideration of their acts.

On the 20th of December the community was startled
with the announcement of the fact that John W. Gully
had been waylaid by some disguised person secreted by
the roadside, not more than half a mile from DeKalb,
and shot from his horse. The animal it appears was
uninjured and went on into town under an empty saddle,
while Gully, recovering from the shock of his wounds —
which were about the chest, and inflicted by two charges
of buck-shot — followed not far behind, on foot. The
news of this cowardly attempt at murder spread rapidly
over the county, and reports were conflicting as to who
had probably done the deed. After the first impression
upon the people in the immediate neighborhood, incident
to an occurrence of the kind, there seemed to be little
feeling of surprise manifested, and expressions like this
were frequently heard:

"Well, the only wonder is that Gully was not killed
long ago. There are scores of men living in the county
who would feel warranted in taking his life in any
possible way."

On reaching DeKalb, where he arrived shortly after
his narrow escape from death on the road, Gully, being
asked who had thus intercepted him, replied that it was
a negro, who was known in the neighborhood, giving his
name. On this statement the accused was immediately
arrested by some of the Gullys. It appeared at once,
and conclusively, that this man could not have been
guilty as charged. Then Gully said it was William
Hopper, a white man who lived near by. Accordingly,
Hopper was set upon by the young Gullys, who found

him at work in a field adjoining the place where their
father had been attacked. But they soon became satisfied that Hopper could not have done the cowardly
deed. The question of course naturally arose, "Who
did do it?" This, perhaps, might have been answered
with some degree of satisfaction by propounding another: "Who, if anybody, had a right to do it?" Gully,
with death and the ghosts of the victims of his own
murderous hand staring him in the face, might thus have
soliloquized.

After a lapse of several days, when it was ascertained
that B. F. Rush had not been seen since one o'clock of
the day on which Gully was wounded, it was rumored,
in a sort of mysterious way, that Gully knew the man
who shot him; but, for reasons which have never yet
been given to the public, he refused to tell who it was, at
least until the March term of the court convened, at
which time an indictment was found against Rush,
charging him with the attempt to murder. As a matter
of course, Gully must then have sworn that Rush was
the guilty man, as there could have been no other
important witness in the case.

Gully's wounds proved to be slight. In a few days he
was upon the streets again, and the attention of the
"citizens" once more called to the great "outrage" of
their arrest by the United States authorities; and on the
fifteenth of January another meeting was called at
DeKalb. Meantime it was secretly whispered about that
Ben Rush was positively known to have been Gully's
attempted assassin, and that he was aided and abetted

by Judge Chisolm, Gilmer and other republicans. Having obtained information of this report, the Judge feared, at the time, the terrible consequences which followed in April of the same year, viz : that a warrant for the arrest of himself, Gilmer and others would be forged, charging them with complicity in the assault upon Gully; that they would all be arrested, confined in jail, and while there, during the session of the great "citizens" meeting, they would be turned over into the hands of a mob and murdered. To prevent this, Judge Chisolm again called around him a number of men upon whom he could rely in any emergency. On the fifteenth, a "large and enthusiastic" crowd of "citizens" assembled, armed with guns, to deliberate upon their grievances. The weapons were stacked in Gully's store, ready for use, and the rioters were only prevented from the accomplishment of their purpose, that day, by the unflinching bravery and bold front of Chisolm and his few devoted followers. Rush, meantime, had not been heard of since the attempt was made upon Gully's life.

Let it be borne in mind here, that the day on which John W. Gully and his followers assailed Judge Chisolm and his wife and children — the 4th of November — a few chosen friends rallied to their defense and remained in the house a greater portion of the day, closely watching the conduct of the mob, thirty-five of whom were afterward indicted. All persons present on that occasion would have been important witnesses in the prosecution under these indictments. Their names are here given : W. W. Chisolm, Emily S. M. Chisolm, Cornelia

J. Chisolm, Clay Chisolm, Johnny Chisolm, John P. Gilmer, Angus McLellan, Charlie Rosenbaum, B. F. Rush, Alex. and Newton Hopper. The reader has already divined the fate of these witnesses.

CHAPTER XIII.

The reader should not lose sight of the fact that, long before the enactment of the barbarous scenes described in the preceding chapter, "home rule and local self-government"—twin messengers of mercy and peace—had been thoroughly established all over the State, and that the dreaded camp fires of republicanism had everywhere ceased to burn. The judiciary, from the supreme court down to the humblest magistrate in a country village, clad in the dignity and majesty of their official robes, looked benignly down in righteous judgment upon the minor transgressions of poor, weak and sinful humanity, and in solemn state passed upon the real intent and true application of constitutional law; while the executive, from the governor down to the beat constable, was left untrammeled to enforce every mandate and decree of the courts. But over and above all, the people, in their simple and unoffending dignity, leaned contentedly upon the strong arm of a legislature which assumed unto itself almost unlimited power to make and unmake at will. No "venal wretch" presumed to lift a voice to ask "why is this so?"

The "good people," those representing all the virtue and intelligence of the State, had solemnly pledged their faith to the restoration of good government, justice and equal rights before the law, and who shall dare to say that "our promises" are not fulfilled?

On the 29th of January, Judge Chisolm, in answer to a summons from the investigating committee, in company with his daughter, set out for Washington. On the 28th, the day before starting, Cornelia wrote to friend as follows:

"We are ready to start for Washington, and expected to have gone to Scooba this afternoon, until yesterday evening, when papa decided that he could not possibly go before to-morrow. I was real sorry I had to wait, for I am growing impatient. ('Hope deferred,' etc.) You don't know the joy I anticipate in taking this trip. The pleasure which new scenes and associations will be to me, however, will not equal the sense of real security and delight I shall feel to know that papa will be free from danger of the assassin's bullet, at least for that little length of time."

While in Washington Judge Chisolm gave the testimony which is quoted in the preceding pages. Himself and daughter spent the winter at Washington and in travel, amid the most agreeable surroundings.

Here is a letter written by Cornelia, at home, shortly after her return — and the last she ever wrote — describing the scenes which absorbed her attention, and in the study of which her time was largely employed while on this trip.

To say nothing of the interest found in the communication itself, it affords more satisfactory evidence of this girl's fine qualities of mind and heart than could be given in any other way.

DeKalb, Miss., April 27, 1877.

My dear friend: I have allowed one bright spring day after another to pass, still leaving unanswered your very kind and very much appreciated letter, until (I'm ashamed to acknowledge it), the fact that it has been on hand a week, forces me to realize how dilatory I am, and animates me to the pleasant task of replying.

Were it possible for me to tell you how delightful a tour I had, or even to convey the faintest idea of how much I enjoyed it, you would think the picture was over-drawn; and if I could write a letter long enough to give you the minutiæ—the most interesting portion to myself—I'm sure you would have many chest-breaking sighs during a perusal of such a missive, were you to have the courage to go over it all. Washington is by far the most beautiful city I saw in all my long journey. Its broad avenues, great thoroughfares, magnificent buildings, lovely parks, and, best of all, handsome gentlemen, combine to make it seem to me a perfect paradise.

Speaking of the buildings, the first and grandest object of interest to the sight-seer is the Capitol, a magnificent structure, conspicuous on entering the city, and prominent for many miles from every section of the neighboring country. It is situated a little east of the center of the city, which has grown more rapidly to the west than was anticipated, and stands on the brow of a plateau ninety feet above the level of the low-tide water of the Potomac. This commanding position was chosen by George Washington. The Capitol grounds are in the form of a parallelogram, and contain fifty-two acres. There is a magnificent conservatory of flowers within the enclosure, and beautiful fountains, which throw the clear, limpid waters from the earth, sprinkling the bright green surface beneath with myriads of dew-drops, sparkling in the sunshine, as though the spot was covered with glittering diamonds. But the principal feature of the grounds is a spacious court on the east front, which approaches from all the avenues and streets leading toward the Capitol. Except where these approaches enter it, the court is bordered by an esplanade, at the rear of which is a continuous seat, from which a view is had of the Capitol. A parapet of pierced stone-work forms the back of the seat, separating it from the green park-like glade. The parapet is broken at intervals by piers, which support beautiful bronze standards, sustaining each two lanterns. The colossal statue of Washington stands in the court facing the east front. It bears the inscription, "First in war, first in peace, and first in the hearts of his countrymen." It was made in Florence, Italy, and you may judge of its exquisite finish when it was under the hand of the artist eight years. Its weight is twelve tons. The dome of the Capitol is, save three, the highest in the world, and from its top may be had the finest view on the continent of the surrounding country.

One of the most pleasant days we spent was the one on which we visited Mount Vernon. We left Washington at ten A.M on the steamer "Arrow" The day was slightly cloudy, with a mystical haze (Hayes) over all things, which gave an air of enchantment to the scenery and made one dream of Paradise. All the bays and inlets which indented the shore seemed like havens of peace and rest, and the white houses peeping through the misty atmosphere. They were far more lovely than they possibly could have looked in the strong glare of the noon-day sun. The Arsenal, with its willow-bordered sea-wall; the St. Elizabeth's Insane Asylum with its turreted red walls, looking like some abbey of the olden land; Fort Foote, perched upon the highest land along the route; the ancient city of Alexandria, or Zelharen, as it was called in the early time, where the old style spire of "Christ Church," of which Washington was so

long a vestryman, is readily identified; Fort Washington,
with its strong embrasures and parapets, mounted with
guns, and planned by Washington himself; and, at last,
Mount Vernon, most sacred shrine of all lovers of liberty.   All were bathed in a gauze-like veil, which hung
like enchantment around us.   We passed many steam-
ers, flying rapidly to and from the capital, while hundreds of sail-boats, of all sizes, floated along in the still
waters like huge birds, sailing with the current.   Landing at Mount Vernon, we were introduced to Col. Hol-
lingsworth, the superintendent of the house and grounds
once belonging to Washington, and now owned by the
ladies of America.   The "Mansion House" looks quite
stately from the river, situated about two hundred
feet above the water.   It is, indeed, the most lovely
place I ever beheld.   To the left of the road, as we go
to the mansion, is a high, well-wooded hillside, abound-
ing in trailing arbutus and other flowers.   About half
the way up, in a small ravine, are several weeping wil-
lows, brought from the grave of Napoleon, at St. Helena.
We were conducted to the tomb, where, in the two
sarcophaghi, inside a vault of red brick, lie the remains
of George and Martha Washington.   From there, we
passed to the old vault from whence the bones of Washington were taken, after the new tomb was built.   We
walked through every room, from the observatory to the
cellar.   In the latter, is a corner stone, with the initials
of Lawrence Washington, who built the central portion
of the mansion, one hundred and thirty-three years ago.
The large painting of Washington, by Peale; the model
of the Bastile, in France, cut from a block of granite,
from the famous old prison; the key of the same, presented by Lafayette; the clothes, camp equipage, water-
buckets, spy-glass, tripod, and many other things were
examined with great interest by our party.   The room
in which the great man died, is between the two south

windows, where they were at that time. The same table, upon which his medicine stood, and, also, that upon which his candle was placed, are in the room; and the old andiron and wire screen at the fire-place.

Our guide told us that when one died in the good old days, in Virginia, the room was closed for two years after the death. Mrs. Washington selected the room immediately above this one—an attic—because, from its windows, she could watch the tomb of her husband. Here she lived for eighteen months, admitting no one but a favorite servant and cat. The corner of the door may still be seen where it was cut out for the ingress and egress of the cat. And here Martha Washington died. We were told she passed the winter without a fire, as there was no way to build one in that room. Is it not probable that this hastened her death?

I cannot begin to tell you the half. I know you are worn out now, so I'll say no more about Mount Vernon; though, did I not know that I'd weary you, I could write about it all day. The whole scene and events of that visit are stamped on my mind more vividly than any I ever passed through. I have spent so much time describing the two places which were most interesting to me, that I must cut the others short.

We witnessed the inauguration; and, oh! it was a a grand scene! I also attended Mrs. Hayes' first reception, and called on President Grant. I attended the theater and opera quite frequently, and "all my cares flew away" while there. I did not see Grace Greenwood to know her, but did see Dr. Mary Walker! Beat that, if you can! Neither did I see Gail Hamilton, but I heard John B. Gough in one of his best lectures, and was at the very door of Mrs. Southworth's rustic, vine clad cottage, where the waters of the Potomac might lull her to sleep every night, and the crowing of the chanticleer at General Lee's old home arouse her every morning, from Arlington Heights, just across the river. I was also in the House and Senate, almost daily, where congregated the finest talent of the land, and where is diffused more eloquence than beneath any other roof in America. I heard Morton, Blaine, Garfield and all my favorites speak.

We went north after leaving Washington, and spent a week in New York city. We also visited the Falls of Niagara. Such a scene beggars description, and makes me feel too plainly how feeble are my powers of speech in attempting to describe a sight so grand. When papa and I first saw the cataract, we could only stand as though riveted to the spot, and gaze, gaze; until it seemed as though we would go over into the mighty waters, so terrible was the flow. We were completely awe-struck; words seemed as though they would be out of place at such a time, and a feeling of reverence, for the Giver of all Good, that He should bestow such gifts upon His unworthy children seemed to creep involuntarily over us. We were loth to leave the spot where we had seen more of grandeur concentrated than was elsewhere to be found. I leave it to your imagination. Oh! that I might ever retain the memory of the scene which met my eyes when I visited Niagara Falls!

I did come home "heart whole," but not exactly "fancy free."

We have been very anxious to send for Lillian, but all the horses are on the farm, and papa can't stop them just yet. I'll be very glad when she can come, for we are expecting the boys — Johnny and Clay — to leave the first of May for St. Louis, where they will take a commercial course, and I'll be very lonesome while they are gone, and Lillian would be so much company for mamma and I.

I'm very impatient to see the twins, too; especially little Rosalie, as you say she resembles her cousin Nelie. I fear I'll be partial to her, though I'll love them both

just as much as I can. Has Alexander grown to be as
large as his father? or, has he passed into oblivion and
given place to his sisters in his father's heart? You said
not a word of him.

If I were to apologize for this long letter, it would
only make it longer, so I refrain.

Papa has gone to Mobile. All are well and join me in
love to the family.

With many good wishes, I am your niece,

NELIE J. CHISOLM.

CHAPTER XIV.

In the month of March, on turning their faces homeward, when the foreboding shadows of the old life in Kemper once more fell across the bright pathway of the joyous girl, it will not be surprising that the precursor of danger again appeared — a faithful and sleepless guardian of unselfish love — and, settling upon her fond heart, called forth the following expression, uttered in tears:

"O I do so much dislike to go back to DeKalb to live; for I feel as though something terrible is going to happen to papa."

From a glimpse of Kemper county society at this time, an entire stranger and one little thinking of evil might well have turned heart-sick and weary away. At that very moment the circuit court for the month of March, 1877, was in session, when Judge J. M. Arnold, by courtesy exchanging with Judge Hamm, a democrat of the strictest school, an officer of high ability and a gentleman of uncompromising integrity, was compelled to doff the judicial robes, and for the time assume the functions more commonly made incumbent upon a chaplain of a penitentiary or an overseer of a house of correction. Ascending the bench, he delivered a lecture upon the depraved and lawless condition of society found among the "good people." John W. Gully had now recovered from the wounds received in December, and, as usual, was at the head of a strong and aggressive faction of his own party; and there being no common enemy to fight, as a matter to be looked for, he had declared war upon the more timid members of his particular faith, and between his own and the opposing factions there grew up an enmity and jealousy as bitter and malignant as that known to have existed against the republican party in its palmiest days. The sheriff, himself an imbecile in the performance of any legitimate duty connected with his office, but a ready and willing tool in the hands of the villainous men who foisted him into it — as will soon appear — had permitted the doors. of the jail to be flung open, and men under indictment for crimes so heinous that bail had been refused even by a democratic judge, were turned loose and allowed to roam the streets at will. The circuit clerk of the county living thirteen miles distant from his office — which he entrusted entirely to a young and irresponsible deputy — was then under a bond of two thousand dollars for his appearance to answer to a charge of embezzlement and obtaining money under false pretenses. The sheriff's deputy — George Welch — who really furnished the brains for running the court house "machine," a sly, unscrupulous and intriguing wire-worker, aspired to become the sheriff's successor in office as against the Gully clan, with John W. Gully at the head, still repining for new fields of conquest. Between Welch and his friends and the Gullys and their friends, there was a jealousy and hatred such as could exist nowhere else under similar circumstances, and it is impossible to divine what would have been the result of this contest had John Gully lived, as indeed it is now impossible to tell what were the immediate causes leading to his death. With this refreshing picture of "home rule" before the somewhat dazed and mystified vision of Judge Arnold, he opened the March term of the court, and on requesting the clerk—or his deputy—to produce the records, lo! and behold, the office had been robbed! Every judgment and civil process usually entrusted to the keeping of the clerk, and every indictment for crime, had been spirited away. The executive and judicial functions of the county had thus been paralyzed; and here was presented the striking spectacle of the people of a whole county, under the reign of "peace and good will toward men," living without law and without order. Judge Arnold, unable to proceed further, adjourned his court until the following morning, for the purpose of gaining time to deliberate upon the situation. He then, through the sheriff, called to order, and, in the presence of the various officers of the county and citizens generally, administered the most scathing denunciation of the shameful and lawless condition in which he had found them—a state, to use very nearly his own words, "of anarchy, misrule and corruption, which, if permitted to go unbridled, would lead to murder and arson, and all the crimes known to the catalogue of infamy."

He admonished the "good people" to waken to a sense of their surroundings, and, for the love of everything dear to humanity, to rally in defense of law and justice trampled under foot. He especially appealed to the board of supervisors and directed them to use every means in their power to bring the perpetrators of this and all other crimes to justice; told them that they should offer a reward of $500 or $1,000 for the apprehension of those who had robbed the clerk's office, and said that he himself would recommend the governor to offer a similar amount. He stated in the course of his remarks, or lecture, that now, under the benign influence of "home rule and local self-government," the people everywhere looked, and, from the fair promises made, had a right to expect better things. That Judge Arnold is a man of far-seeing judgment and close observation, will be shown by the events which followed upon the scene just described.

By this masterly stroke of villainy, murderers, thieves, robbers, house-breakers, swindlers of every grade, and malefactors in office, were turned loose upon the community, and to-day are plying their various avocations without let or hindrance. Some eighty-five criminal and forty civil processes were thus lost. M. L. Naylor, a magistrate, indicted for misdemeanor in office, was thus set at liberty, and the grand jury, of which Phil Gully was foreman, failed to re-indict in this, as indeed they did in nearly or quite all the cases where a member of the great party of reform was in any way involved.

Some months before, the merchandise of M. B. Wood & Co., a firm doing business in Scooba, was attached by their northern creditors, who suspicioned them of fraudulently disposing of their goods. In certain cases of attachment the sheriff has authority to demand a bond of indemnity from the plaintiff. It was believed that good and sufficient bonds in the case were given, but on coming up in the circuit court — September term of that year — the sheriff objected to the bonds, alleging that the sureties, for various reasons, were insufficient. Upon this a warm and prolonged controversy arose between the lawyers employed on either side. Finally the court adjourned until the next day, when it was found the sheriff had dissolved the attachment, as the statute gives him power to do, when, in his judgment, sufficient indemnity is not offered. Thus the plaintiff was defrauded of his just dues. The plaintiff's attorneys, believing this act on the part of the sheriff to have been fraudulent and illegal, made a motion before the court charging the same, and claiming damages of the sheriff, on his sureties, for the amount of plaintiff's whole claim, amounting altogether to eighteen or twenty thousand dollars. It is the opinion of some of the best attorneys of East Mississippi — those employed at the Kemper county bar — who are familiar with the facts, that the sheriff, Sinclair, could and would have been held responsible for this large sum of money had not the robbery of the clerk's office been procured, and every paper in the case stolen and destroyed. By the theft of these papers alone, then, one of the most villainous swindling schemes of the age was perpetrated.

Under the conciliatory policy, as indicated by the message of the newly inaugurated president, the whole power of the State government being under control of the " best citizens," Judge Chisolm indulged the

fond hope that a spirit of greater tolerance would prevail, and that possibly he might be permitted to return
home, and there remain unmolested until such a time as
he could dispose of his property and leave the country
forever, which it was his settled determination to do.

On the 29th of March, the father and daughter arrived
at DeKalb; he to resume the accustomed routine of
business on his plantations, and she once more to become
the central star, around which the hopes and aspirations
of the household clung in the fondest admiration and
love.

The delight experienced by the fond wife and mother,
on the return of her loved ones, knew but one cloud, and
that was the ever present fear that assassination would
overtake her husband, before he could settle his business
and get away.

Possessed of an amiable and contented disposition,
it was the good fortune of Cornelia to be able to make
the most of her surroundings, and she was not among
those to sit down and repine at any condition, however
displeasing it might be in fact; and a few days later she
sent a friend in Washington by letter, the following
cheerful and animated picture of her daily life. The
message bears date DeKalb, April 22, and is addressed
to her "Dear Flora." Only a brief extract is given:

"This afternoon, brother and I mounted our horses and
galloped away for a ride. We left the road about five
miles from town and took to the woods, and I would
tell you how beautiful they looked, if I could. The
trees are all clothed in a soft, tender foliage—the leaves

being about half grown. There are lovely flowers of
every color and variety now in bloom along the creek.
Brother and I dismounted, and *galloped* on foot through
the woods for an hour or more. I will send you a little
bouquet of wild flowers that I picked by the creek,
down at the fish-trap, on papa's plantation. The banks
there are very steep and high, and the stream being now
much swollen by rains, the water dashes over the trap in
a perfect cataract. The beautiful yellow jessamines meet
across the stream, and clasp their soft, sweet blooms and
tendrils together; while the banks are gemmed with
forget-me-nots, buttercups, wild violets, dogwood and
honeysuckle. Oh, I wish you could have been with us,
on our ride; then you would know how delightful it
was. It is getting quite late, and I'm sleepy. * * *
Sweet papa just returned from St. Louis, yesterday, and
is going to Mobile this week. He sends his kindest
regards. * * * Remember me to your mama, with
love.   Your affectionate friend

NELIE."

But to the household generally, the time passed with
the usual monotony of country life, save only the
excitement incident to the preparations being made to
send the two older boys, Clay and Johnny, to school at
St. Louis. The Judge had been to Mobile for the purpose of negotiating with his merchants there, for funds to
defray the necessary current expenses. In the afternoon
of the 26th of April, he returned with the money and
suitable equipments for the boys, and the tickets for
their transportation to St. Louis in his pocket. Coming

up the open common, in front of the house, the Judge
was first greeted by Cornelia, who, running down the
pathway, threw her arms around his waist and kissed
him, and the two walked to the front gate, where they
were met by Mrs. Chisolm, and together all passed on
to the house, taking seats on the front porch, where they
were soon joined by the three boys. While there
engaged in conversation concerning the future, and dis-
cussing the probability of their soon being able to leave
DeKalb, and go to some place where greater security to
life, and the pleasures of friendly intercourse with their
fellows might be found, John W. Gully rode by on the
accustomed route to his home, about a mile and a half
out of town. He had been from sight but a few minutes, when a negro came riding hurriedly up from the
direction in which Gully had gone, and reported that
Gully had been waylaid and shot, and was then lying
dead in the road, but a short distance from his own door.
The shock which this sudden and terrible intelligence
brought to the happy little group just described, can
better be imagined than told; but certain it is, not one
of the family from the father down, bitter and malignant
as Gully's enmity toward them had been, who did not
shed tears of sorrow and regret. Sorrow for the murdered man and his afflicted family, and regret that they
were compelled to live in a community where such terrible crimes were permitted to go without the shadow
of investigation by the courts of the country.

CHAPTER XV.

This was on Thursday, and event followed event in rapid succession. For some reason never yet explained to the satisfaction of any one except the enemies of Judge Chisolm, and very much contrary to the custom usual in a climate like that of Mississippi, Gully was not buried until Saturday, the 28th. And here it becomes necessary to introduce a new character in the progress of this story, and one whose significant name will be closely allied with the darkest phase of the infamy now to be disclosed. At the burial, a large crowd of citizens had assembled from all parts of the county. George S. Covert, who had married a niece of Gully, and lived in Meridian, a distance of thirty-five miles from DeKalb, appeared upon the scene, and became the central figure in the conspiracy which was there consummated. Covert was from the "city," wore a clean linen shirt, and words from his mouth fell upon the ears of the savage horde like an inspired revelation. These men, quick enough at best to inaugurate a scene of debauch and riot, and ready at all times to credit any story, no matter how false and groundless against a political opponent, were told by Covert and his wife's kindred, that Ben Rush was Gully's assassin; that he had been hired to do the deed by Judge Chisolm, who was then at his home in DeKalb, and now an opportunity had presented itself in which they could rise in the majesty of their might, and rid the county and the world of this man. Nor must they undertake so hazardous a task alone. Chisolm, they well knew, would fight with that desperation and strength which a consciousness of right and a determination to defend his home and his children to the last, would lend him, and numbers sufficiently large to insure success without danger to themselves must be gathered. Accordingly a courier was dispatched to Ramsey Station, in Alabama, and the aid of their old confederates in blood invoked. The Alabamians, it appears, were somewhat loth to respond to this call, unless some more plausible excuse for riot and murder in open day could be shown, and we are thus spared the pain of adding another horror to the long list of their terrible deeds.

To give character and tone to the statement already circulated, implicating Judge Chisolm in the murder of Gully, it was told at the funeral that Rush had been seen but a short time before by two negroes—George Fox and Dee Hampton—at night, in a saloon in company with Chisolm and Gilmer, when in the very act of concocting the scheme for the assassination, and all the time Rush held in his hand the fatal shot-gun with which his work was to be accomplished. To this was added the story that he had secretly met Judge Chisolm, while the latter was at Mobile, when the barter and sale of death was finally agreed upon, and the money actually paid to Rush. The ghost of this man Rush, whose destruction Gully himself had so many times sought, would never "down." Rush, who singly and alone, in open battle, had faced the whole murderous Gully clan, was the only one upon whom they could, with any degree of plausibility, fasten the guilt of John W. Gully's untimely taking off. Upon this point alone their case rested; for, through no other device or subterfuge could they reach the object of their especial hate and fear. Chisolm was the real murderer, and Rush the guilty agent. This theory must be established or their case fall to the ground. Upon this theory Covert claimed to be acting under advice of eminent counsel from Meridian. A case against them could be sustained far enough, it was believed, to accomplish the original design, and quench their thirst for blood. But this work, it was agreed, must be effected without danger to themselves. What was done must be done quickly, and time should not be taken for reflection. If, by any means, Chisolm should become apprised of their purposes before his arrest and confinement had been accomplished, they well knew he would call around him again, as in times past, a few devoted and heroic men, upon whom an assault could only be carried at a most alarming sacrifice to the assailants. The better to secure the object of the conspiracy, Gilmer and Rosenbaum, who lived at Scooba, and the two Hoppers living at DeKalb, were to be taken simultaneously with Judge Chisolm, disarmed, and together all to be locked up in jail. The arrests must be made under the forms of law and the promise of protection, else they would not be tamely submitted to, and these men, when thus warned of danger, would be left to band together at will, in defense of their lives and homes. All the work that remained, after the cell doors were fastened upon the victims, could be done easily and with no risk. The accomplishment of this, then, became the great strategic point; and to George S. Covert was mainly assigned that delicate and refined piece of villainy. If the Meridian *Mercury*, a newspaper published in his own town, is in any way to be credited, Covert had recently met with unparalleled success in keeping a bosom crony out of the penitentiary by means of bribery, false swearing and the like, and it is not surprising that the Gullys should have made choice of this one of their numerous relatives, whose rare genius in the art of deceit and perjury had been so well established, to assist them through a similar means, in getting Judge Chisolm and his associates locked up in jail, where they might be burned or shot to death as circumstances presented. Before these men could thus be arrested and confined, a warrant, or something having the appearance of a warrant, authorizing it, and based upon a solemn oath, must be presented. Covert, though not valiant in the use of the shot-gun, was ready in the performance of this work, and J. L. Spinks, a justice of the peace—the same of whom mention is made elsewhere—himself undoubtedly knowing its full purport and meaning, issued the warrant which is copied below, *verbatim et literatim :*

STATE OF MISSISSIPPI, ⎱ ss.
   Kemper County. ⎰

To the sheriff or any constable in said county greeting :

Whereas, Geo. S. Covert has this day made complaint, on oath, to the undersigned, a justice of the peace in and for the county, that he fully believes and has good reason to believe that B. F. Rush did, on the night of the 26th inst., kill and murder John W. Gully, and that W. W. Chisolm, Alex Hopper, Newt Hopper, J. P. Gilmer and Charlie Rosenbaum were accessories to the deed. Wherefore we command you to forthwith apprehend the said B. F. Rush, W. W. Chisolm, Alex Hopper, Newt Hopper, J. P. Gilmer and Charlie Rosenbaum, the accused, and bring them before T. W. Brame, Esq., or some other justice of the peace of said county, at DeKalb, on Monday, the 30th day of April, 1877, to answer the above charge, and do or receive what, according to law, may be considered touching the same, and have you then and there this writ.

Witness my hand and seal, April 28, 1877.

(Signed) J. L. SPINKS, J. P., [SEAL.]
Kemper County.

STATE OF MISSISSIPPI, }
    Kemper County.   }

Before me, J. L. Spinks, a justice of the peace, in and for said county, personally came Geo. S. Covert, who stated, upon oath, that he fully believes and has good reason to believe that B. F. Rush did, on the night of the 26th inst., in said county, feloniously kill and murder John W. Gully, and that W. W. Chisolm, Alex Hopper, Newt Hopper, J. P. Gilmer and Charlie Rosenbaum were accessories to the deed; whereupon he prays that warrants be issued for their arrest, and they be made to answer the charges brought against them.

(Signed) GEO. S. COVERT.

Sworn and subscribed to before, me April 28th, 1877

(Signed) J. L. SPINKS, J. P.

WITNESSES:—J. J. Griffin, S. Evans, Esq., Jno. W. Smith, J. R. Smith, Dr. Edwards, M. Rosenbaum.

The following indorsements were found written across the back of this warrant:

"THE STATE OF MISSISSIPPI
vs.
B. F. RUSH,
W. W. CHISOLM,
ALEX HOPPER,   } WARRANT.
NEWT HOPPER,
J. P. GILMER, and
CHARLIE ROSENBAUM.

Rec'd in office April 29, 1877.
(Signed) F. C. SINCLAIR, Sheriff."

"I hereby appoint W. W. Holsel my legal and special deputy, to execute and return this writ according to law.
April 29, 1877.
(Signed) F. C. SINCLAIR, Sheriff."

M. Rosenbaum, whose name appears above as one of the "witnesses" to the murder of John W. Gully, has been for twenty-five years one of DeKalb's most honored and respected citizens. He is the father of Charlie Rosenbaum, one of the accused, and upon his honor as a gentleman, declares that he never was approached by Covert, or any one else, in regard to the killing of Gully; that he knows nothing whatever of the facts, and that his name was there used without his knowledge or consent. "Dr." Edwards, whose name, even, they did not know, and J. R. Smith are residents of Meridian. They have both been life-long friends of Judge Chisolm, and make the same declaration in regard to their connection with the pretended warrant, and their knowledge of the guilt

of the accused parties, that Rosenbaum does. The
names of the two negroes, it will be borne in mind,
do not appear on the warrant as witnesses at all.   John
W. Smith and S. Evans are the attorneys under whose
advice Covert acted, if his own statements are to be
relied upon.   Smith lives in Meridian and Evans at
Enterprise, distant thirty-five and fifty-five miles, respect-
ively, from DeKalb and the scene of the assassination
concerning which their names are written down as witnesses.   What they proposed to testify to has never
been divulged, as the warrant does not appear ever to
have been "executed and returned according to law."
But what signified an act of false swearing to a man like
Covert, with a soul not only void of honor, but human
sympathy as well.

The warrant, as will be seen, was issued, or claimed to
have been issued Saturday, and made returnable before
Esquire Brame, in DeKalb, on Monday.   This early
return was arranged to meet any doubt which might
arise in Judge Chisolm's mind as to the danger of delay
after his arrest, whereby a crowd of ruffians might be
assembled for the object of taking the law into their own
hands.   He would then expect to pass over the Sabbath
in custody.   Meantime, by the quick despatch of couriers
to every portion of the county, at the dead hour of
night, through dark and unfrequented bridle-paths, across
streams, lagoons and swamps — the old familiar routes
so often traveled by these men in days gone by, when
their mission had no worse significance than the
whipping or killing of some poor negro or teacher of a

public school — willing hearts and hands could be gathered at DeKalb early on Sunday morning, sufficient in numbers to guarantee their ability to murder two or three men already disarmed and securely locked up in jail, awaiting the process of a judicial investigation, and that without incurring much danger to themselves.

This was the plot by means of which the great work, so many times defeated, was finally to be accomplished, and in which George S. Covert, an "honored and respected citizen" of Meridian, appeared as the great overshadowing genius.

CHAPTER XVI.

All night long the sound of iron hoofs rang out upon the motionless air, soon to be rent by the murderous discharge of guns, mingled with the shouts of savage men, the shrieks of despairing women and affrighted children, whose prayers and tears and warm life-blood were to add fresh fuel to the unbridled flame of hate and fury. All night long, girt about with pistol and leathern belt, and guns across the saddle's pommel, the grim-visaged and grinning barbarians rode into DeKalb by twos, threes and fours. Before the soft and genial rays of the sun of early spring had kissed away the dew of that beautiful Sabbath morning, two hundred and fifty men, reared in the most degrading ignorance and trained in a school of blood and crime, were hovering about the environs of DeKalb, ready to do the will of any one who might assume leadership.

They had not long to wait. Sinclair, the imbecile sheriff and ready tool of the conspirators, with two deputies, had already gone, fortified with his forged and fraudulent warrant to the house of Alex Hopper, and placed him and his younger brother Newton under arrest. Hopper expressed unwillingness to go with the sheriff until he had breakfasted, and the sheriff reluctantly consented to wait. During this delay, Hopper clandestinely sent a note by a negro to inform Judge Chisolm that he himself had already been arrested under a charge of complicity in the murder of John W. Gully, that the sheriff and his deputies would next visit him for the same purpose, and that warrants were also out for the arrest of Gilmer and Rosenbaum. This, as will be seen, afforded Judge Chisolm ample time to have escaped, if he had desired it, and which he certainly would have done had he felt the gnawings of a guilty conscience. His wife and children, with quick intuition, accustomed as they had been to scenes of danger and outlawry, knowing well the spirit that possessed the hearts of the men who were thus seeking to place their beloved guardian within a mesh from which escape would be impossible, implored him to mount a horse and leave at once. To this Judge Chisolm replied that he had nothing to fear; was innocent of any crime or offense against the law, and that for no consideration would he incur the suspicion of guilt by leaving his home, or in any way trying to avoid any just and legal process. While his breakfast was being prepared, his wife sent a servant to the stable for a horse, thinking that possibly the Judge might yet be prevailed upon to go. She also ordered a cup of coffee to be placed upon the table in advance of the regular meal, and with all the earnestness of her nature, begged her husband to drink his coffee, and then mount the horse and fly from the certain and inevitable death which awaited him.

While the mother and daughter were thus beseeching, the sheriff and deputies, with the two Hoppers, came up, and the warrant produced in the preceding chapter was handed him to read. Judge Chisolm willingly submitted to its decree, but objected to being carried to jail, where he had reason to believe he would be murdered, and asked that a guard might be placed over him at his own house. To this the sheriff at first objected, stating that "they say you must go to jail." By this time a number of men had gathered about the house, and the sheriff consented to leave his prisoners there, in charge of men appointed, until they could have a hearing the following morning. Judge Chisolm named some of the persons whom the sheriff designated as guards, and he then despatched a courier to inform Gilmer and Rosenbaum of their contemplated arrest, advising them to come to DeKalb, and give themselves up peaceably as he had done. Men in greater numbers, with guns in their hands, continued to assemble around the house from every direction. Finally, without a reason being given for so doing, Judge Chisolm was removed to a small building apart, and in which there was no fireplace, and composed of thin weather-boarding, having no lock or other means of fastening the door. On passing into the room, the Judge for the first time saw that his premises from every quarter were occupied by armed men, while others stood in the streets leading by.

He asked the sheriff the meaning of all this, and his reply was that, "*They* say your guard must be increased." Mrs. Chisolm then came in and protested against her husband being confined in a damp room, without fire, as he was otherwise in poor health and subject to asthma. The sheriff then consented to the prisoner being conveyed back to the house, and, as they

were passing the open space in the yard, between the
building in which he had been temporarily confined and
the dwelling, a large crowd of villainous looking men
rushed in a body, with guns in their hands, and surrounded him. The Judge again asked the sheriff if this
was the usual mode of treating a prisoner when in
charge of the proper officers of the law. His only reply
was, "*They* say that you must be securely guarded."
Judge Chisolm then asked who he meant by "*they.*"
Was he the sheriff of the county, acting under the
proper requirements of the law, or was he simply
the instrument of a mob, which only sought the life of a
defenseless victim? To this no reply was made, and in
a few minutes, after first going out upon the streets and
holding a conversation with a man named Jere Watkins,
who had just ridden up from the rear of Judge Chisolm's
house, at the head of a large body of armed men, and
who is known to be a most notorious Ku-Klux des-
perado and villain, the sheriff returned and told Judge
Chisolm that he must now go to jail. "*They* say you
must go to jail," were the exact words he used. Mrs.
Chisolm then asked the privilege of being alone with her
husband a few minutes before he left, and, without waiting for the sheriff's consent, she went with him into an
adjoining room, where she opened a closet from which
there was a trap-door leading into a garret above. She
then besought her husband to take refuge there; that
she would hand him his guns, and he could defend himself against the whole cowardly horde, and if finally
killed, which she believed was more than probable, he

would not die like a felon, but his last breath would be drawn in his own house, where he would be surrounded by his wife and children, who worshipped him. This he also refused to do, stating that he had submitted to the mandates of the law, and that he must wait and obey its processes. Besides, if he were to secrete himself in the house, as the mob knew he was there, when the shooting began, his wife and children would probably be sacrificed and the building burned down over their heads. Without further hesitation he placed himself in the hands of the sheriff and his guards—none of whom were those originally selected by Judge Chisolm—and the procession moved toward the jail. The Judge's wife, and the children, Cornelia, Clay, Johnny and Willie, all followed close by his side.

Before leaving the house, Angus McLellan, a brave and sturdy old Scotchman, and a subject of Great Britain, who had stood by Judge Chisolm through many a trying scene before; kind and gentle as a woman when not aroused, but determined as fearless when in defense of that which he conceived to be the right, came in and volunteered whatever assistance he might be able to render the distressed family; and, arming himself with Clay Chisolm's gun, followed them to the jail. When near the door at the foot of the stairs leading up to the cells, the sheriff stopped Mrs. Chisolm and refused her admission. She insisted, and, despite his efforts to prevent, went up, as did all the children and McLellan.

Meantime Gilmer and Rosenbaum, who had received Judge Chisolm's note, set out for DeKalb, in compliance

Angus McLellan

with his request to come in and give themselves up to the sheriff. Gilmer, when preparing to leave home, took off his watch and all valuable papers about his person and gave them to his wife, and while at the glass, arranging his toilet — with which he took more than usual pains — he said to her, "Effie, if I were to die suddenly, you would not have me buried until certain that I was dead, would you?" To this she replied "no," and then, holding her little child in her arms, she went up to her husband, and with tears in her eyes, begged him not to go to DeKalb; or, if he would go, to take her with him. Having no conveyance ready at the time, Mr. Gilmer could not grant her request; but told his wife that if he was sent to jail she could come up late in the evening and remain with him until his release, which he felt sure would take place the following day. They proceeded on their journey, and when about half way to DeKalb, Gilmer and Rosenbaum met a deputy sheriff who had started to Scooba for the purpose of arresting them.

This man said nothing about making an arrest, but when aside with Gilmer, showed him the warrant and told him as he valued his life not to go to DeKalb at all that day. But they rode on, and when arriving at the residence of Mr. M. Rosenbaum, father of the young man alluded to, they stopped and sent a note in to the sheriff, stating that they were there and would remain subject to his order. This was about twelve o'clock. James Brittain, a citizen living near, who had been deputized by the sheriff, came, took them into custody and started to the jail. As they passed along the streets squads of armed men fell in at intervals from every accessible point. The two prisoners began to show signs of uneasiness, when Brittain took Gilmer by the wrist, and while thus holding him, one of the Gullys emptied a charge of buck-shot into his back between the shoulders. Gilmer exclaimed :

"O ! Lord; don't shoot any more ! I gave myself up and you promised to protect me !"

He then broke loose and attempted to run into a narrow alley, between two buildings, but was confronted at the other end of the passage by a crowd of men and there shot down and his prostrate body riddled with bullets. That evening, before leaving home, while preparing to follow her husband to DeKalb, his mangled and bloody corpse was laid down at Mrs. Gilmer's feet.

Rosenbaum appealed to a friend whom he recognized in the mob — none of them were disguised — and through his assistance kept out of range of the guns which were frequently leveled at him, and was in that way carried on to the jail, where we left Judge Chisolm and his family but an hour or two before.

CHAPTER XVII.

Gilmer was already dead, and the young widow with her orphan child, and Gilmer's aged mother, paràlyzed with grief, were bending over his cold and inanimate form. Chisolm, Rosenbaum and the two Hoppers were now securely locked up, and no friend of either bore arms save the dreaded Scotchman, McLellan. All the work which had been assigned to Covert and his aids, was thus successfully accomplished, and that worthy had already withdrawn to some safe retreat. He was himself the father of a blooming family, with young daughters just budding into womanhood. Doubtless he did not care to linger where the screams of women and children, mangled, torn and bleeding, would soon rend the air, and, like a poisoned and barbed arrow, strike deep into his cowardly and guilty heart. Now this much was done, before the final slaughter began it was desirable that the alleged proof of the complicity of these men in Gully's murder should actually be produced. Where no proof is known to exist, in fact, in some countries the process of manufacturing it is slow and often impossible; but not so in others. At least, a process which had before served well in many a case on record in Mississippi, and which had seldom failed, was left the people of Kemper.

The two negroes, who were reported to have seen Chisolm and Rush in their mysterious nightly vigils when concocting the scheme of murder, were to be compelled so to testify; and now that the confinement of Judge Chisolm and his friends prevented the possibility of interference on their part, Fox and Hampton, the pretended colored witnesses, were taken into a wood, near by, and hung by the neck for the purpose of enforcing them to testify to something which they never saw or heard. Knowing nothing, as a matter of course, they told nothing, and, after having been strangled and beaten nearly to death, were permitted to go, and the alleged proof has never yet been found.

Within the dark and frowning walls of the county jail, shut up with common thieves and prisoners of the lowest grade, from an early hour on that Sabbath morning until the sun had sunk well-nigh down the western horizon, the doomed family waited, and watched and prayed; while without, three hundred yelling savages, like hungry wolves, were clamoring for their blood.

The quick, sharp report of a dozen murderous shot-guns from up the street, and the subsequent appearance of Charlie Rosenbaum, who was thrust into jail like a felon upon the scaffold; the loud curses and yells of the infuriated mob, all together, told too well the fate which had befallen Gilmer.

Inside the jail, the pretended guards would put down their guns, and pass out and in at will. Many of these were men who had known Judge Chisolm and his family well for years; and not a few of them had, for as long a time, been pensioners upon his bounty. Among others, Phil Gully came in and spoke of the many acts of courtesy which had passed between himself and Judge Chisolm in days gone by. At one time the guns were stacked in a corner, and nearly all the guards went out, when Cornelia discovered that some of the pieces, at least, were loaded only with blank cartridges. She told her father that in case the guards did not come back, he might have to withstand a siege, and in that event would need amunition, and expressed a desire to go to the house for the purpose of getting it. To this the father objected, at first, fearing that she would meet with insult, and probably personal harm in passing through the mob without. She insisted, and after getting consent of the jailor to pass, under the pretense of going for food, took her little brother Willie, and together they went to the house. While there, she gathered up all the jewelry, silver-ware and other valuables, packed them securely in trunks, locked the trunks and carried them into closets, which she also securely fastened; then secreting powder, bullets and wadding under her skirts, took some provisions in her arms, and with Willie returned to the jail, and there informed her father that the servants had all taken flight, and that the premises were deserted. Judge Chisolm then expressed a desire that the stock, especially the horses, should be watered and otherwise cared for. In the excitement of the morning they had been entirely neglected. Not one of the family cared to go, fearing that an assault upon the jail would be made during their absence, and the bloody work of the mob accomplished. The Judge was particularly anxious concerning the horses, apparently having a faint hope that they might yet in some way be of service to him. Mrs. Chisolm concluded that she could best be spared from the jail, and asked Johnny to go with her.

This little fellow, thirteen years of age, as tender and delicate as a girl, had often been made the subject of pleasant jest by other members of the family, on account of retired manners, taste for books of an elevated moral tone, and strong passion for the cultivation of flowers. But on that day his true character was developed, and rose to a height in courage and devotion worthy the emulation of the most exalted hero.

In reply to the request made by his mother, he said, his eyes filling with tears:

"O, mother, I don't want to go, for as soon as I leave they will kill father. But if you say I must, I will go!"

Then taking little Willie the mother went to the stable, and, while attending to the stock, the report of the dreaded shot-gun again rang out upon the air. Running through the yard to the gate in front of the house, in plain sight of the jail, she saw two or three guns discharged at a man then on the side facing her. When the smoke cleared away he had sunk upon the ground. Calling out to Willie to hurry on, that another man had been killed, Mrs. Chisolm ran across the common toward the spot. When half way there, fearing that an accidental shot might kill her boy, she told him to hide in a deep ditch which they were then compelled to cross. Taking a second thought, and believing they would kill him any way if found, she told him to go to a negro cabin, situated on the left about a hundred yards distant. The boy did as he was told, and Mrs. Chisolm hurried on to the jail. In passing, she recognized the dead body of McLellan, the one whom she had seen two of the Gullys in the act of shooting but a moment earlier, while she was at the gate. Before Mrs. Chisolm left the jail for the stable the sheriff came up and demanded of the old Scotchman that he should go down stairs; that in refusing he was resisting the legal authorities of the county. McLellan replied that he had never disobeyed a law in his life; that if the *law* required of him that he should leave the jail he would go, and the old man reluctantly and sorrowfully put down his gun, went below and for some time stood in the hall, at the foot of the stairs, leaning against the wall with his head down, in a thoughtful and abstracted mood. While passing out, on her way to the stable, Mrs. Chisolm saw him standing as above described. After she had gone the sheriff, according to his own testimony, went to McLellan and repeated his demand that he should leave. In compliance with this the old man went through the door—the only outside opening in the building—which is on the south side, and passing around the east end of the jail, went to the north side; and while walking in the direction of his own house, his head still down, he was fired upon by the Gullys and his body riddled with bullets.

At this time, Cornelia, who stood looking through the grates of a window at the ghastly scene below, fully conscious of the impending fate of her father, in the very agony of despair, fell upon her knees and begged that a single spark of mercy might be shown them. "O! why do you do my papa so bad?" she cried. "He never has harmed any one in his life, much less any of you, so many of whom have taken food from his hands!"

"—— —— him!" exclaimed Bill Gully, who stood below with a gun on his back, "we'll do him worse than that!" and this, with a half dozen shots fired at the window at the same moment, was the reply she received. The blood of the old Scotchman had given fresh impetus and courage to the mob; for, by his death the last dangerous obstacle that interposed between them and the victim whose life they most craved, had been removed, and they rushed furiously into the jail, headed by Rosser and the Gullys. With superhuman strength Mrs. Chisolm worked her way through this crowd to the door at the head of the stairs. This door opens into a hall which leads entirely around the jail, outside of the cages or cells, which are built in the centre. In this corridor, directly back of the stairway, Judge Chisolm had taken refuge. Within the door stood Cornelia and Johnny, with Overstreet and Wall, the only remaining guards. Finding the door fastened, Rosser, with loud and angry oaths, called for an ax, and cursed his confederates who feared to come up the stairs. One ax was brought and then another. Mrs. Chisolm, seizing Rosser by the arm, implored him to desist, and asked if he did not have a wife and children at home. To this he made no reply, but rudely thrust her aside and vigorously plied the ax. Cornelia entreated Overstreet to shoot through the grates in the door at Rosser and the mob coming up the stairs. Overstreet replied that he dare not; stating as a reason that he knew his own life would pay the penalty of such an act. He begged them, however, to go back, but to no purpose.

The numbers around the door increased, and guns were thrust through the grates and fired into the hall at random. Judge Chisolm, seeing that his time drew near, then cried out, "Daughter, bring me some guns from the corner; I know I must die, but I will go down with my colors flying!" Seeing that the door must soon give way, Cornelia then took up an armful of guns left by the guards, who had deserted their posts, and carried them to her father. Coming back to the door, she was just in time to receive the contents of a load which, first striking the flat, iron grating, filled her face with chips of lead and burnt powder, causing the blood to flow from more than a score of ugly wounds.

Despite the frantic efforts of Mrs. Chisolm, who never ceased to labor and pray, the lock was chopped out and there stood Rosser and Bill and Henry Gully, with guns ready for use. Cornelia and Johnny, with a courage scarcely ever before recorded in the annals of great and chivalric deeds, endeavored to hold the door back against the fearful odds. But steadily it gave way, and Rosser's gun was put through the opening and discharged, shooting off Johnny's right arm at the wrist. So close was the muzzle that his clothing was set on fire. At this the little fellow screamed out, in the agony of fear and pain, and Clay came and carried him behind

one of the iron cages; but was no sooner back to the
door, where he went immediately, than Johnny had
returned and placed his shoulder against it, and with all
his little strength sought to hold it back. Finally, with
a sudden crash, the door flew open and Johnny ran into
his father's arms, crying out as he did so, "O! don't
shoot my father!"

Cornelia then seized Rosser's gun and interposed her
fast-failing strength against the monster.

"Go away," cried he to the girl, "or I'll blow your ——
brains out."

"For shame!" said a fellow at his heels, "would you
shoot a woman?"

"Yes, —— her!" was the reply; "I will shoot any one
that gets in my way!"

Then, with terrible force, he hurled the frail girl against
the wall, and no further power remained between Rosser's second barrel and the special object of his rage save
the slender form of the innocent boy. His weapon was
leveled, and the bullets went crashing through Johnny's
heart. Judge Chisolm, seeing his boy thus murdered in
his arms, seized the gun left by McLellan and sent its
contents into Rosser's head, scattering his brains against
the wall. At sight of all this, and from loss of her own
blood, Cornelia, feeling faint, ran back to her mother,
who had not yet been able to get through the door, as
the opening was filled with men who were firing down
the passage-way at random, in the direction whence the
shot came that had killed Rosser. In the meantime
their own bodies were out of range, and consequently

out of danger. Charge after charge of shot, fired in this manner, was emptied into the solid wooden casing around the cells, and there the deep, ragged gashes remain, sickening mementoes of the darkest infamy and most disgraceful cowardice ever recorded of beings wearing the human form.

Seeing their leader fall, these miserable creatures quailed under the steady gaze of that one man at bay, and fled like frightened sheep, dragging the dead body of Rosser down the stairs by the heels, and the stairway and hall below were cleared in an instant. The mingled blood and brains of this poor wretch were left on every stair, from the top to the bottom of the jail.

Up to this time Mrs. Chisolm did not know that Johnny had been killed, and before the mob fled, she reached through the grates, and placing her hand on Cornelia's head, tried to give her words of encouragement; told her to think of her "poor papa," whose life, if she continued to be brave, might yet be saved. Again the fainting girl rallied and ran to her father, whom she found bowed down over the body of his murdered son, Just at this moment the mother and Clay came up, and together all sank upon the floor, and there over the body of that young and martyred hero there went up a wail of agony and despair, such as is seldom heard on earth.

No time could be lost in weeping. As long as life lasted there was hope, and Mrs. Chisolm, as quick in expedient as she was brave in the defense of those she loved, tried to get her husband into a cell where she could exchange clothing with him, thinking he might thus escape in disguise; but this was found to be impracticable, as no unoccupied cell could be opened.

While her mother and father were thus engaged, Cornelia lifted up the dead body of little Johnny, put out the fire which was still burning the clothing on his shattered arm, and then laid the arm carefully across his bleeding breast; kissed again and again the pale cheeks and lips; prayed God to give him breath to "speak to sissy once more," and then, with her handkerchief, wiping up the last drop of his precious blood from the floor, she carried the lifeless body down the hall and placed it behind a cage, where it would be, for the time being, secure from further violence.

Baffled, defeated and driven from the jail, the cowardly mob knowing that there was but one man to resist them, dare not renew the assault, and a stratagem worthy of savages was resorted to. At once the cry of "Run them out!" "the jail is on fire!" fell upon the ears of the doomed family. The hall already filled with smoke from the burning wads and gunpowder, the prisoners confined in cells, believing that the jail was already in flames, began to howl like wild animals in a burning amphitheatre, making the whole a scene to have equaled in horror Milton or Dante's most extravagant conception of hell itself; and it was believed by all that the building would soon be enveloped in flames. Sooner than remain, Cornelia said to her father, "Oh! papa, see how easy poor Mr. McLellan died; it is much better for us all to go down and be shot to death, than to stay here and be burned alive!" It was then decided to descend the stairs, and take whatever chance of escape might be offered. Mrs. Chisolm and Clay, with the dead body of Johnny, led the forlorn hope, while the Judge, with a gun in his hands and Cornelia's arms around his waist, followed close behind. Mrs. Chisolm and Clay made the landing below without interference, and laid their sorrowful burden upon the floor, but the Judge and Cornelia were met before reaching the foot of the stairs by Henry Gully, with a gun already presented. Here was another door with iron grates, and after seeing the immediate danger that threatened her husband, Mrs. Chisolm shut this door, while Cornelia shielded her father's body with her own, at the same time pulling him down out of range, and there, with one arm around his neck, the hot, scalding tears mingling with the blood that ran down her girlish cheeks, she cried out, "Oh! Mr. Gully, if you must have blood, I pray you to take my life and spare my darling papa, who has never done you a wrong."

This appeal was answered with a charge of shot from the monster's gun, which struck a heavy gold bracelet on the girl's arm, cutting it in two, and driving a piece of the ragged metal deep into her wrist. A bullet passed entirely through, shattering the bone from the wrist nearly to the elbow. The same charge grazed Judge Chisolm's neck in several places, and cut off a small portion of his nose. Gully then stepped back for another gun, when Cornelia, still clinging to her father, opened the door and came on down. They had no sooner reached the foot of the stairs than the assault was renewed with increased fury. Still this frail girl, shot and bleeding from a score of wounds, clung with one arm around her beloved father, while with the other hand she pushed aside the guns which were leveled at his breast. Where, in any account of remarkable filial love, unselfish devotion or great physical daring in woman, do we find a picture like this? Nothing short of the Divinity, which is said to have raised up a Joan of Arc, could inspire a courage and heroism like that displayed by Cornelia Chisolm throughout that fatal day.

At this time the two Hoppers and Charlie Rosenbaum were permitted to come down without arms, and turned loose in the street with the threat of instant death if either of them sought in any way to release or defend Judge Chisolm. The three escaped without injury.

CHAPTER XVIII.

While Mrs. Chisolm was struggling with the mob at the outside entrance, Bill Gully came up and deliberately shot at her twice, but a merciful Providence seemed to protect her, as neither load took effect. Mrs. Chisolm then seized the gun which had been brought down the stairs by her husband, and discharged both barrels at Gully. The wadding struck him full in the breast and fell harmless to the ground. This was one of the guns furnished the guards by the sheriff and left by them up stairs. It was loaded only with blank cartridges.

At the suggestion of his wife, Judge Chisolm now turned to walk down the hall in rear of the stairs to take shelter behind a pile of goods belonging to Mr. Gilmer, which had been taken from him by the sheriff and there stowed away. Before this cover was reached, Phil Gully stepped out from a door opening into the hall, and, with a heavy hickory stick uplifted — the same that he carries to-day — advanced toward Judge Chisolm, as if to strike him down; but, by this time, shots had been fired into his body from front and rear, and Phil was deprived of the satisfaction of giving the finishing touch to this scene in the drama; for the Judge, at that moment, sank upon the floor, begging that he might be carried to his house and not permitted to die like a felon in jail. Believing that their work had been fully accomplished, the mob left, and coolly awaited further developments from the outside.

While Mrs. Chisolm was bending over her husband's prostrate body in momentary expectation of catching the last words that fell from his lips before the spirit took its flight, the Judge, in a low whisper, said: "*My precious wife, I am about to die; but, when I am gone, I want you to tell my children that their father never did an act in his life for which they need to blush or feel ashamed. I am innocent of the charge these men have preferred against me, and have been murdered because I am a republican and would live a free man!*"

Cornelia, who, in the melee before descending the stairs, had been struck in the face by some brutal hand, which, in addition to the gun-shot wounds already received, had blackened and disfigured her countenance in a horrible manner, now went to the door to beg for assistance to carry her father's and little brother's dead bodies home. This appeal was answered by a shot which struck her below the knee. Fifteen large duck-shot and one buck-shot were thus lodged in her leg, while another passed through the counter of her shoe into the foot. This was overlooked in the multiplicity of her other injuries and never was discovered until after her death, though before that time her heel had become very much swollen and inflamed, when upon examination of the shoe the place where the shot entered was found. A missile of some kind also struck her hip, causing a severe and painful sore. Her bonnet strings, which were tied in a bow knot under her chin, were nearly severed by a shot which thus narrowly missed her throat. These ribbons only hung together by the hem on one side, three separate balls having passed through them. Thirty bullet holes were counted in the skirts of her clothing, which was a mass of blood, from the little silk hood she wore on her head, down to her shoes. On receiving the last charge she ran back to her mother exclaiming, "O! mamma, they have shot me again!" This was the first and only exclamation she made throughout, concerning her own wounds. Mrs. Chisolm then went to the door and in turn begged for assistance, while Cornelia stood bleeding over the inanimate forms of her father and brother. Presently a young man stepped forward from the mob and volunteered his services. Mrs. Chisolm, still in full possession of her quick faculties, said to him, pointing to the body of her husband, "Sir! did you do that?"

"No, madam," was the reply. Then pointing to her dead boy and bleeding girl she asked, "Did you do that?"

"No!" was the second answer; "I have not discharged a gun to-day."

"Then," said the heroic woman, "your touch will not pollute the dead bodies of my darlings, and, if you will, you may help me to carry them from this terrible place!"

Stooping down, Mrs. Chisolm raised her husband's head and placed his arms around her neck. Clay lifted his feet, while the young man took hold in the middle, and together they started for the house, not more than a hundred yards distant. When out of the jail they were joined by Bob Moseley — better known as "Black Bob" — a man whom Mrs. Chisolm and Clay both knew very

well, and whom they had seen foremost among the rioters throughout the day. Loathsome as his presence
was, they permitted him to become a bearer in the
mournful procession, as they could not well proceed
without him. When about half the distance to the
house there arose a fresh cry from the mob, whose
vengeful thirst, it appears, had not yet been fully satisfied. "He is not dead yet," they said; "let's go and
finish him!" Seeing them come, headed by a brute
named Dan McWhorter, Cornelia lingered behind, and,
as they came up, with her shattered arm raised to
heaven, she declared that her father had died before
leaving the jail, and besought them not to mangle his
dead body. By this declaration and appeal they were
deceived and turned back.

Reaching the house, it was found locked and the servants all gone. A small window from a back porch was
broken open and the Judge's helpless body dragged
through it into the house. With no domestics, and
everything securely locked, great difficulty and delay
were experienced in finding anything for the relief of the
wounded. Dr. McClanahan, a near neighbor and life-
long friend of the family, although a feeble old man,
came in and rendered all the assistance in his power.
With the aid of two negroes he carried home the corpse
of the murdered boy, Henry, Gully remarking to him as
he gathered the body up, "Doctor, I have killed your
best friend, meaning Judge Chisolm. Cornelia was
placed upon a low bed, in the same room with her
father, and while Mrs. Chisolm was busy preparing

something for their comfort in another part of the house, Bob Moseley returned, and uninvited walked into the room where the victims lay. Cornelia, believing that he had been sent back by the mob to ascertain if her father was really dead, or likely to die, rose from the bed and drove him out of the room. It was subsequently ascertained that he did, in fact, return for the purpose divined by the girl, as his confederates, it has since been learned, condemned him for having aided in carrying the dying man away, knowing that life was not yet extinct, Moseley was therefore desirous of reinstating himself in their confidence and esteem. Besides, he had been once admitted into the house, and was, they believed, a suitable person to return for information concerning the extent of Judge Chisolm's wounds, which, if not fatal, were to have been made the signal for another attack.

On examination, the Judge's worst wound was found in his left hip, where a full charge of buck-shot entered from the rear.

Several different men living in DeKalb, all of whom were known to have been active participants in the conspiracy, came to the house that evening, and, professing friendship and sympathy, offered their assistance. As might be supposed, their offers were rejected. Dr. Fox, the only competent surgeon in the place, or anywhere within immediate reach, was known to have been one of the instigators of the riot, as he had been a counselor, if not a member of the Ku-Klux in days past; and as a matter of course none of the family would voluntarily place themselves within his power.

Thus they were shut out from sympathy or aid, save that which came from a few friends, the greater number of whom were beyond reach, on account of the distance they lived from DeKalb, or because of the barriers which the threats of the mob interposed.

Those who came were faithful and true, but unfortunately but few were skilled or experienced as nurses, and what made the situation still more alarming, the necessary means for relief or comfort were not always to be obtained.

About ten o'clock that night, Judge Chisolm's two brothers, John and Marbury, and two or three of his young nephews arrived from the southwest beat, a distance of twenty-two miles, to which place a courier had been despatched for them by the Judge early in the morning, when his arrest was first made.

Some hours before their arrival, Henry Rosenbaum, a brother of Charlie Rosenbaum, in answer to a despatch sent him in the morning at Meridian, had gone to Scooba and thence to DeKalb. On arriving at the scene of the massacre, he proceeded at once to Judge Chisolm's house, where he rendered every assistance possible. He had come to DeKalb in anticipation of aiding his brother.

All of these friends had been compelled to travel by an unfrequented and circuitous route; were all day on the road, and knew nothing of the terrible fate of the family, until their arrival at Judge Chisolm's house, too late to render such material aid as they would gladly have done. All that could be, with the means at hand, was done for the sufferers through the night, and early on the following morning the despatch which is copied below was sent to Meridian:

"SCOOBA, MISS., April 30, 1877.
Received at Meridian, April 30, 8:15 A. M.
To Capt. J. M. Wells:
Come to us immediately, by the way of Scooba, and bring the best surgeon you can get. Brother Johnny is murdered, and father will die. Sister is badly wounded.

H. CLAY CHISOLM."

Up to the time of the receipt of this despatch in Meridian, the reports concerning the massacre were wild and conflicting; the anxiety with the few who sympathized was great, while the excitement incident to the terrible affair in a neighboring town, where most of the parties concerned were well known, was general. The despatch was answered at once, as follows:

"To H. C. CHISOLM, DeKalb, Miss.:
No train this morning; will bring surgeon across the country immediately.

J. M. WELLS."

Two different surgeons whom the writer requested to go, made excuses of one kind or another. Finally Dr. John D. Kline was asked, and at once consented, but afterward sought an opportunity of getting from some prominent democratic citizen a letter of introduction, a passport or safe-guard of some kind, against molestation by the citizens of Kemper, while on his way to DeKalb, and a guarantee of protection after his arrival. This he obtained from a gentleman well known and highly esteemed by the Gullys and their co-workers. Even after this precaution, the doctor objected to going with the writer, as the latter was well known in DeKalb as a political and personal friend of Judge Chisolm. An effort was then made to find some one whose known friendship with the Kemper County murderers would afford protection. There were many of this kind in Meridian, but out of the dozen or more who were approached, not one would go. There was in Meridian at the time, however, an under-current of strong and earnest sympathy for the distressed family. At last a colored barber who had once lived in DeKalb, and who knew the road well, volunteered to go as a driver, and with him Dr. Kline started across the county, while the writer took the first train for Scooba, arriving in DeKalb the next day, after having ridden from Scooba thirteen miles through the country. The doctor reached Judge Chisolm's house at ten o'clock that night, and found the condition of the father and daughter not so iminently dangerous as had been at first reported. More than twenty-four hours had passed since the wounds were inflicted, however, and it was impossible to probe Judge Chisolm's wounds, to ascertain their full extent, yet the physician and all friends of the family were encouraged to believe that he might recover. A thorough examination was made of Cornelia's injuries, which she bore without a murmur. They were severe and exceedingly painful, but no one at the time believed them fatal.

The next morning Mrs. Chisolm, herself, prepared little Johnny's body, which had lain in the parlor alone over night, for the grave. The coffin came from Scooba, and after carrying the body to Cornelia's bed-side, she kissed the pale cheeks again and again, when it was placed in the coffin, and Willie, accompanied by two or three friends — all who could be spared from the house — took it off and buried it. A prayer offered at the house by the agonized mother, was the only service held.

The same day Judge Robert Leachman, with two ladies — Mrs. Christian and Miss Caskin — friends of Cornelia, arrived from Meridian. They, however, could not remain but a short time, and that same day the doctor himself was obliged to return.

In the shadows of death, like birds of prey, they hovered nigh, impatient of the final dissolution, and hearing repeated threats of a renewal of the attack by the mob as soon as they should find that Judge Chisolm was not likely to die from the wounds already received, a close watch was kept at night from without, while a dozen loaded guns were always ready for use within. For better security, planks were nailed up at the bed-room windows. The mental strain and anxiety incident to all this, together with the inability to secure prompt and constant medical attendance, materially lessened the chances for recovery, and it was determined to remove the patients to some place of safety as soon as a force could be raised sufficiently large to insure the success of such an undertaking.

But this it was found difficult to do, as Judge Chisolm's friends living in the county, who had attempted to come to the assistance of the sufferers, had, in many instances, been stopped on the highway and made to turn back, so that now very few ventured to come. Mrs. Griffin and her sister, Miss McDevitt, were the only ladies in DeKalb, outside of the political friends of the family, that ever pretended to approach the house. They came constantly and rendered invaluable assistance. A young man living some distance in the country, although a democrat, visited the house once and volunteered to assist in guarding it, or in taking the patients to some place of safety. Another gentleman, a resident of DeKalb, and also a democrat, came several times in the night, and under cover of the darkness stole away, fearing to have it known that he sympathized with them in their affliction.

About the third day Governor Powers arrived from Macon. The Governor remained but a day or two, when he returned, determined, if possible, to raise a posse and send them to our assistance. Before Governor Powers left, however, J. M. Stone, the governor of the State, came. He told the writer, while sitting on the steps of Judge Chisolm's house, that, after thorough inquiry among all parties, he had been convinced that there was a conspiracy existing in the county for the purpose of taking Judge Chisolm's life; that he did not believe there had ever been found a particle of proof showing the complicity of the murdered man with the killing of John W. Gully, and that in his belief the very warrants for their arrest were false and fraudulent. He further stated he did not believe that Judge Chisolm was free from the danger of another attack by the mob, if once it was thought he was likely to recover or get away. On being asked if he could do anything in the way of assuring the family protection while they might remain, or a safeguard in moving, he replied that he could only direct the sheriff to appoint a special deputy, who might be selected by Judge Chisolm or any of his friends. Under this deputy a number of guards, sufficiently large to insure protection, and chosen in the same manner, might be placed at his disposal. To this the reply was made that there was nothing to select a guard from, for the very good reason that all the friends Judge Chisolm had within reach were already enlisted, and they needed no appointment from an imbecile and villainous sheriff. Beside that, the experience with guards, taken from among the citizens of Kemper county generally, within the past few days at least, had been such as to warrant us in not again voluntarily placing him or his family under their protection — which would most likely be such as vultures give to lambs.

CHAPTER XIX.

The patients both grew weaker from day to day, and Cornelia was removed into an adjoining room. Her solicitude for the welfare of her father knew no rest up to the hour of his death, and often was she quieted with the promise that on the following day she would be carried to his bed-side; but as often were we obliged to disappoint her, as she was never in a condition to be removed.

The physician did not return from Meridian until a peremptory order was sent for him. What were the influences that kept him away no one ever knew. The wounded had then suffered three days without any skilled attention.

Within five days from the date of the tragedy every mail that came brought letters of condolence and sympathy, most of them coming from entire strangers, but many written by the friends and admirers of the bright and joyous girl whom she had met while on her visit to the North. From the Northern States, especially, the warmest letters came, while the newspapers of that section thundered the indignation felt by the people in tones which could not be misunderstood.

It was the privilege of the writer of this to open and read many of these letters, and in the lonely hours of Cornelia's prostration, they were a source of great satisfaction and delight to her. Many of them, at her request, were replied to at once and the answers read to her. Then her face would light up with a sweet smile as she would say, "Now lay them carefully away, and some day, if I ever get well, I will answer them all myself."

A few of these letters, given here, cannot fail to interest the reader, as they are a further proof of the feeling and sentiment of the people in that section of the country from which they came; and it is a great gratification to me and to all the friends of the martyred dead, to be able to place upon record here the fact that human nature is not everywhere dead to that boasted sympathy which has so often been falsely claimed for it.

WASHINGTON, D. C., May 2, 1877.

My Dear Miss Chisolm:

I have read the newspaper reports of your sorrows with a sad heart, and hasten to express my sincere sympathy. My husband regarded your father as one of the kindest hearted men living, incapable of injuring his worst enemy. In conversing with Judge T. this morning, he made the same remark, and said it was impossible that your father could in any way be connected with the assassination.

I have been thinking of the last time I saw you; you remarked "I was never so happy in my life," and now to think of the contrast. What can I say to comfort you? Words cannot express the deep sorrow and sympathy I feel for you at this moment. If I could only be with you—take you in my arms and try to soothe your sorrows, how gladly would I do it—but words are cold. I can only commend you to lean on Him who loves you better than earthly friends, and whose tender love and compassion will never fail you. In all my own troubles this has been my comfort, that "Like as a father pitieth his children, so the Lord pitieth them that fear him."

How is your dear mother? No doubt well nigh crushed by her many troubles. As younger and stronger, a double duty falls to you; that of tenderly caring for both father and mother. I pray that you may have strength for the burden thus suddenly laid upon you.

After you are calm enough to write I would like to hear all about the matter; in the meantime please inform me, by postal card, what are the probabilities in your father's case? Will he recover? I most earnestly pray that he will. Assure him of my confidence in his perfect integrity and innocence. Judge T—— wishes me to convey to you and your family his sympathy in your terrible affliction.

I was disappointed in not again seeing your father and self before you left Washington; but felt sure that you failed to find my residence.

My kindest regards to your father and mother, and much love for your own dear self.

Lovingly yours,

Mrs. J. L. R.

This excellent letter was followed within a day or two by another from the same kind author. The two were read to Cornelia, and at her request the subjoined, written at the bed-side of the patient sufferer, was sent in reply. This communication soon after found its way into the newspapers of the country, and will be recognized, no doubt, by many readers:

DeKalb, Miss., May 12.

Madame: At the request of Miss Nelie Chisolm, whose wounds render it impossible for her to write, I serve as her amanuensis. She takes great pleasure in acknowledging the receipt of your kind letters, which have come to hand since the DeKalb horror took place, and let me assure you your kindness is appreciated. I have had the pleasure of opening your letters and reading them to her, and from your writing judge that you do not know the brave and devoted little daughter was shot, beaten and mangled equally with the father. Her right arm was shot through and through while endeavoring to shield her father. A whole charge of buck-shot, which first hit the flat iron bars of the cell, struck her full in the face, filling it with chips of lead and burnt powder. A blow in the face from some brutal hand has blackened and disfigured it in a fearful manner. She was also shot in the leg below the knee, and is now lying prostrate and helpless as an infant, and nothing but the tenderest care and best surgical aid can save her arm and precious life. Her father is still alive, but suffering intensely; yet we have some hopes of his final recovery. The house is being guarded by a few faithful friends and relatives; but we do not know at what hour the savage barbarians may renew the attack. You can do us all no more good at present than to lay the enormities of this massacre before the people at Washington, especially the President.

All of these kind letters touched a responsive chord in the hearts of that household, and will never be forgotten. The effect produced by them will remain with those who listened to their hopeful greetings so long as the name of Chisolm shall be perpetuated.

PHILADELPHIA, PENN., May 2, 1877.
JUDGE CHISOLM:

In behalf of myself and fellow members, of one of the most influential republican clubs in this city, permit us, one and all, to offer to yourself and noble family our heartfelt, sincere sympathies in this your hour of

distress. Would to God we could offer you material protection and effective aid. Be of good cheer; keep up
a stout heart; and may Heaven hear our prayers for
your safety. The indignation with which we received
the news of the murderous attack upon your gallant
little band, has not yet subsided, and were the distance
not so great you should sit beneath the shadow of
fifteen hundred breech-loading rifles, (the number of our
club). Oh! for just a few minutes' *interview* with those
cowardly miscreants who think it so chivalrous and
brave to murder defenceless Union men. Let them
remember that although "the mills of God grind slowly,
yet they grind exceeding small," and that the avenging
goddess will, at no distant day, blot them out. The
people here at the North are beginning to talk as they
did in '61, and it is among the possible things to have
"Sherman's march" repeated.

If you, or any of your family, will communicate to me
a full and fearless account of the events in which you
have all been such prominent actors, my thanks will be
of a substantial nature. A friend at my elbow has
suggested that if you are in need of fire-arms, be good
enough to give us the name and address of a trusted
friend. In the meantime, we all hope for your speedy
recovery, and if there is any way in which we can serve
you or yours, do us the favor to make it known at once.
Pardon this disjointed epistle, for I am laboring under
some excitement from having just finished the details of
your martyrdom, which will account for my rambling
thoughts and tremulous chirography.

Accept, again, our sympathies and well-wishes, while
our prayers, we trust, are registered above for you all.

Yours sincerely,   V. P.

The above was responded to at the time by the
request of Judge Chisolm himself and other members of

the family. Here is the reply to it, which was afterward
printed in a Philadelphia paper, with editorial comments
as follows:

"THE MARTYRED CHISOLM FAMILY.

"Throughout the length and breadth of our land the
hearts of patriotic men and women now turn with deep
and heartfelt sympathy to the lonely and broken-hearted
widow, who in her desolate home in Mississippi, grieves
with a sorrow none can know, and feels most keenly
that life is indeed a burden, with naught of happiness
for her. Mrs. W. W. Chisolm now mourns the death of
a favorite son, a beloved and accomplished daughter and
a noble and affectionate husband. In the agony of her
grief she surely is almost tempted to cry unto God and
say, 'my trials are indeed greater than I can bear.'

"We cannot give full expression to our thoughts as
we reflect that the dead are the victims of political
hatred; have been hurried to untimely graves because
of the political opinions of the head of the family.
Surely their martyrdom will give inspiration to loyal
men to move in solid column for all time to come, and
never cease in their efforts on behalf of liberty and the
republic until every traitor is driven from the land, or
made to bite the dust at the hand of avenging justice.

"The story of the attack upon Judge Chisolm, the
heroic defense on his behalf by his daughter, is too well
known to our readers to call for repetition here.
Wounded, she died for want of proper surgical and
medical treatment, which was denied her by the inhuman

mob which surrounded her.   He, too, now sleeps the sleep of death.

"The following letter, written to a prominent citizen of this city, is given to our readers, but, for obvious reasons, the names of both the writer and the recipient are withheld.   As will be noticed, it was penned before the death of the Judge and his daughter:"

DEKALB, MISS., May 9, 1877.

*   *   * *Philadelphia, Pa.:*

Dear Sir: On behalf of Judge Chisolm and his bereaved and afflicted family I acknowledge the receipt of your favor of the 2d inst., tendering them sympathy and encouragement.

Be assured, my dear sir, that the good wishes and thoughtful solicitation of the Republican Club, as expressed in your letter, are well understood and thoroughly appreciated, and every word therein contained finds lodgement in warm and responsive hearts.

As I write, the widow and orphan child of one of the victims of the massacre is sitting near by — Mrs. Gilmer — almost forsaken by her kindred, whose sympathies are with the murderers of her husband.   It is needless for me to say she is utterly broken-hearted.

The members of the Judge's family who still survive (himself and heroic little daughter) are both lying before me, writhing under the affliction of a score of ghastly wounds.   Both are doing even better than we could have hoped, though the Judge's life is despaired of.   The daughter will probably recover, carrying through life a maimed and crippled hand.

Little Johnny, with one arm shattered to pieces and his heart shot out, is sleeping quietly under the ground. The house is being guarded by a few faithful friends and relatives, who are well supplied with shot-guns and revolvers, and will struggle to hold out against the fearful odds of "home rule and local self-government."

The family stand in no immediate need of assistance of any kind; yet God only knows how soon they may be stripped of all earthly goods, and themselves, with others, driven like beasts to the woods and there murdered.

We shall be pleased to hear from you at any and all times, and would gladly detail the full particulars of this bloody affair, which, in all its plottings and final consummation, is more diabolical, cowardly and inhuman than the Mountain Meadows massacre itself.

You can probably do us no greater good just now than to aid in every possible way to spread the horrors of this affair before the northern people, and at the same time let us all pray to God that the "hope" of a renewal of Sherman's march may yet be a reality. Again thanking you, I will close. ✳ ✳ ✳ ✳

BRISTOL, PENN., May 8, 1877.

DEAR MISS CHISOLM:

In your great sorrow, affliction and bereavement, which must be almost insupportable, silent sympathy with you, on our part, would probably be better; but for the reason that we know that no earthly comfort can avail, would we write commending you and yours to the merciful care and support of our Heavenly Father. He will not utterly desert us, though allowing us to be sorely afflicted and bereaved.

We have prayed for you constantly since learning all, that God, in his infinite mercy, may restore your father to life, and succor and enable you to get away from that dreadful country.

I wrote to the New York *Times*, and hope that a thorough investigation will take place, and a severe punishment be meted out to the murderers and assassins. Some time they will get their deserts, you may rest assured. God's hand is not shortened!

Bear up in this great trial of your life, our dear friend. Do not give way to despair, but commit all to God, and light and comfort will come at last.

Be assured of our deepest sympathy; and the Lord take care of you and yours, is the fervent prayer of your sorrowing friends,   MR. AND MRS. T. H.

NEW ORLEANS, May 6, 1877.

CORNELIA CHISOLM:

Respected Miss : Please excuse the liberty taken to address you. I am very sorry to hear of the death of your father and brother. I hope you are not badly wounded. Should you need any assistance let me know, and I will do all in my power for you. I am a republican and a gentleman, in every sense of the word. Should you be in need of a home, my house is at your service.

Wishing you may soon be well, allow me to remain very respectfully,   G. M. L.

SULLIVAN, ILL., May 21, 1877.

MISS CHISOLM:

Please pardon my boldness in thus addressing you, but I could not resist after reading an account of the troubles lately in your place. My desire is to find out whether or not the enclosed account is true. I had the pleasure of visiting your town in 1874, looking out a location, but was not entirely satisfied with the climate. You will confer a great favor on me if you will give me the facts regarding the matter enclosed; and I further assure you not one word will be made public without your consent.

Please honor me with a reply. Very respectfully,
                    T. B. S.

NEWPORT, R. I., May 13, 1877.

MISS CHISOLM:

Pray do not consider it an unpardonable liberty when I, unknown, write to you to express my deep admiration of your brave conduct. I trust, with all my heart, it is not necessary for me to add words of condolence. Please pardon me, for I believe I shall feel better all my life for having even *so* much to do with such a brave, devoted daughter. But if my writing is to be excused, I suppose it must be because it needs no notice, so I shall write no more. Believe me, I am yours, very humbly,

H. T. C.

LINCOLN, NEBRASKA, May 15, 1877.

MISS CORNELIA CHISOLM:

Dear Friend: Although an entire stranger to you I trust that I may yet address you as friend.

I have just been reading, in a Chicago paper, a description of the dastardly assault made by the mob upon your father, and of the heroic resistance made by him and yourself. Although my own work in this world is to repeat the proclamation made by the angels to the shepherds on the plains—"Peace on earth, good will to man"—yet I felt a good degree of satisfaction when I learned that at least one of the mob had been made to bite the dust. Surely those men must have been dead to all sense of honor and to all the finer feelings of human nature. I have read many accounts of mob violence practiced upon the poor negroes in the South; but I do not remember to have read one that equalled in inhumanity this assault upon your father.

It is my sincere hope that your wounded father is still alive and that he may entirely recover. It is sad to lose a parent, but doubly sad to lose one by the hand of savage men.

You will pardon me for saying it, but your heroism on

that occasion has challenged my admiration. Few
young ladies would have had the nerve to face a crowd
of such desperate men. But you did it in devotion to a
father whose life was dear to you as your own, and for
this I honor you. I sincerely hope that your wounds
may speedily heal, and that your brave right hand may
not be seriously or permanently injured.

As I read the account of the brutal deeds of those
men, and of their threats of further violence, my heart
was touched, and I wished earnestly that I might be of
service to you in your hour of sore trial.

If these lines, hastily written, will in any degree
encourage you I shall only be too glad. If I could help
you in any other way I would do so. Be assured that,
though a stranger, and hundreds of miles away, my
sympathies and my prayers are with you.

Your friend,   S. M. C.,
Pastor Bapt. Church.

FORT DODGE, IOWA, May 17, 1877.

MISS CORNELIA CHISOLM:

I have just read in the New York *Tribune,* of May
11th, an account of the most atrocious barbarism it has
been my lot to read in connection with southern politics.
Will you kindly allow me to tender you my profound
sympathy, and to express the hope that happiness may
still be in store for your wounded parent. Your conduct
I cannot sufficiently admire. I have seen few women
whom I think would have had the courage you displayed. I trust your wounds may be speedily cured and
no permanent injury to yourself be sustained. Again
allow me to express my appreciation of your noble and
heroic conduct. I am yours respectfully,

CHAS. E. T.

TERRE HAUTE, IND., May 10, 1877.

MISS CHISOLM :

I have read with the deepest interest Mr. Smalley's account, in the New York *Tribune*, of your heroism and sufferings, and I cannot refrain from offering you a stranger's appreciation and sympathy. Such rare courage as you have shown must awaken the deepest interest everywhere in the North. I know from personal experience the depraved condition of society in parts of your State, and I can comprehend somewhat the trials through which you have passed. Pardon me if I intrude upon your grief; I only want to say a kindly word which will tell you that you have many friends whose faces you have never seen. If you could spare the time, at a later day, to send me a line, telling me of the result of your own and your father's injuries, you will receive the gratitude of one who, though a stranger, will always be your friend. O. J. S.

The answer to the above afterward appeared in the Terre Haute *Express*. It is copied below :

DEKALB, MISS., May 14, 1877.

Dear Sir: I am requested by Miss Nelie Chisolm and others of the family, to return thanks for your kind favor to them of a recent date. Your expressions of sympathy and regard are highly appreciated, and at some future time, should the life of the poor girl be spared, she will take pleasure in acknowledging her gratitude in some more substantial manner. Her father died Sunday evening last, at eight o'clock. She is yet unconscious of the fact, and her physician says that the only hope for her is in keeping the terrible truth to ourselves. It is beyond the power of language to describe the affliction and distress which has been experienced in this family since that dark and bloody Sabbath. The savage coolness with which the plot was matured for the destruction of the victims, is not surpassed in the annals of crime since the beginning of the world. While Mr. Smalley's letter contains some truths, when taken as a whole it is a farce, and I am surprised that a Northern man, coming here upon the ground, should not have taken some pains to obtain the whole truth, and, obtaining it, have the manhood to publish it.

Judge Chisolm had as noble and true a heart as ever beat in the breast of man. He was judge of probate of his own county before the war, and was re-elected to that responsible position by the unanimous vote of the people immediately after its close. He has raised an elegant and refined family, and what better proof do you need of their appreciation of his virtues and goodness, than to know that every one of them, from his innocent little boy thirteen years of age, up to the tender and delicate wife, followed him to the jail, where he had been induced to go by connivance of the sheriff, under promise of a safeguard; and then, under the shadow of its blackened walls, when they were assailed by three hundred yelling savages, fought for the husband and father with a desperation and heroism which ought to have palsied the most brutal arm. The sight of the little daughter, shot, beaten and mangled in a most shocking manner, is proof enough, it seems to me, to convince the world that there must have been something in the heart of the father, now dead, better than ordinarily falls to the lot of man.

The work of that Sabbath day is the culmination of a scheme which has been on foot here for seven years, and for no other purpose than that "democracy" should have ascendancy in the county. The scenes enacted here on the twenty-ninth of April are liable to be repeated anywhere in the State when any considerable number of republicans may see fit to organize. If you could have any sort of conception of the indignities and dangers through which Judge Chisolm and his family had to pass last fall during the canvass, to say nothing of every preceding canvass for the past seven years, you would be compelled to relinquish at once all hope or faith in a government tolerating such enormities.   *   *   *

EAST MISSISSIPPI FEMALE COLLEGE,
MERIDIAN, May 13, 1877.

MY DARLING FRIEND:

Don't censure me, please, for not writing to you before. I expect you have thought it strange that the one who professed herself to be your greatest and truest friend has forsaken you in the hour of darkness, when the clouds of trouble hung thickly o'er you and your devoted family. Believe me, Nelie, the reason I have not written before is, that my heart was too full of sorrow, and I felt bowed down with such excruciating pain to think of my loved friend suffering so much. Indeed I sympathize with you deeply. It is with anxiety that I hear your hand is worse; you must be suffering agony. If I could be with you and help care for you. I understand that the Christians have been very kind. It requires misfortune to show us our true friends. I heard of your bravery with great pride, for I understood so well your affectionate love for your father, and knew so well how outraged you felt. These are mere words, yet they come directly from my own heart, but they seem void when compared with what I would express. If it was in my power I would come to you at once. This you know is impossible, as our school soon closes, and so much is expected of me. Nevertheless, I hope I will be able to see you anyway as soon as it does close, which will not be long. All the girls sympathize with you deeply, and desire me to assure you of their sincerity. I will write soon again, my darling. May the Lord, "who keepeth His people in the hollow of His hand," watch over you and your afflicted family during this time of trouble, and provide for your comfort; for "He doeth all things well." Believe me your ever devoted friend.

ANNIE.

MERIDIAN, MISS., May 16, 1877.
My dear suffering friend:

The telegraphic wires brought us the doleful and heart-rending news, yesterday, of our sweet Cornelia's death. We had previously heard that her father had left us. Oh! what a woe is thine, my darling friend!

This is to let you know that in all of your sorrow I have been grieved, and have been to the altar with the petition that the Healer will be with you and enable you to "pass under the rod" with safety, with your armour brightened and your sandals buckled on, ready for the future contest with the evil one. Dear madam, I pray that this mountain of your troubles may flow down like a plain at His bidding, who holds in his hand the destiny of nations; and cordially join in St. Paul's prayer that this present affliction, which is but for a moment, will work out for you a far more exceeding and eternal weight of glory.

Ah, me! what shall I say about my dear, sweet child, Cornelia? I can't write about her. I will only say, come expressive silence and tell my woe; for, if I had the pen of an Archangel, I could not make known what I feel.

Mrs. L—— and all the children join me in tendering to you and your two children their heart-felt sympathy. Mrs. L—— requested me to say to you if she could possibly leave home, at this time, she would gladly come to your house and try and console you by her presence. Poor F——! she was so hurt about our dear Cornelia.

We heard, yesterday, that Captain Wells was sick. I do trust that it is nothing serious. Give him my kindest regards. I hope he will soon be well again.

With my prayers for your future happiness, I will have to sink silently into a signature,   M. S. B.

WASHINGTON, D. C., May 23, 1877.

MRS. W. W. CHISOLM:

Dear Madam : I do not write expecting to be able to speak to your sorrowing heart any words of consolation, or to say anything which will lighten your heavy burden of grief, but I want you to know that the people of the whole country grieve with and for you. I have just received a letter from a gentleman in Ohio, who called with me upon your late husband and daughter while they were in the city. The gentleman begs me to write you and ask for your dear lost daughter's picture, and I assure you it could not be given into more worthy or patriotic hands. If you can do so, will you not send me one also? I want to show it to the Secretary of War, with whom I am somewhat acquainted. I called upon the President, Attorney-General and Secretary of War, while you were surrounded by that terrible mob which prevented you from taking your loved ones to a place of safety. Before any decisive steps could be taken, a hand more powerful than a mob released them. We mourn with you for them, and for you in your great sorrow. If it is not too sad a task, will you write me? If you have a picture of the Judge, will you send it to me? I will take it to Brady and have his portrait hung among the nation's honored dead. My friend from Ohio, Mr. S. M. L., who wants Miss Cornelia's picture, is a personal friend of the President and General Garfield. I hope I may sometime see you, and be able to speak of the many pleasant hours I spent with your dear ones here in Washington.

Hoping to hear from you soon, and that you will have strength to bear your terrible affliction, I am your friend in a mutual sorrow,   MRS. H. H. S.

CHAPTER XX.

Up to the hour of her death Cornelia would spurn with contempt any good wishes tendered her that did not carry with them the same feeling for her father, and the very last act of her life was to tear out the leaves of her autograph album on which were written the names of young gentlemen whom she had reason to believe were in sympathy with her father's enemies.

Six or eight days had passed when Capt. Shaughnessy and Major McMichael, friends of Judge Chisolm, came from Jackson. A plan was then entered into for carrying the wounded to some place where they might at least be free from the fear of a night attack by the mob, and accordingly Mrs. Chisolm addressed the following appeal to Governor Stone:

To HON. J. M. STONE, Governor of Mississippi:

Sir: Believing you to be humane and desirous of preventing the needless effusion of blood, I most humbly and respectfully appeal to you for aid in protecting my husband and children, until such time as I am able, with those of them whom God in his mercy may spare to me, to leave the county and their home. If you can aid me in behalf of my wounded and dying husband and daughter, I would ask that Capt. M. Shaughnessy, of Jackson, be authorized to raise a body of men sufficiently large to protect and remove us to some place of safety. Respectfully,

MRS. W. W. CHISOLM.

This letter Capt. Shaughnessy carried with him to Jackson, where he hoped to meet the governor. On his arrival there he found that Mr. Stone had gone to Natchez, and to that place Capt. Shaughnessy then despatched the contents of the letter, to which the governor replied by telegraph as follows:

To M. SHAUGHNESSY, Jackson, Miss.:
I cannot consent to your proposition to go to Kemper county with a body of armed men. I will return as soon as possible. J. M. STONE.

Ready to take advantage of any circumstance, no matter how trifling, to detract from the real facts concerning the outrage, and, as it would appear, add to its horrors by persecuting any one who might openly express a feeling of sympathy for the sufferers, a scurrilous article charging Capt. Shaughnessy with duplicity in manifesting so much interest in their behalf, came out in the Vicksburg *Herald*. To this editorial Capt. Shaughnessy replied through the columns of the *Commercial*, another paper published in the place, branding the charge as false and infamous. His reply resulted in a challenge from Mr. Charles Wright, editor of the *Herald*, to fight a duel. The proposition was promptly accepted. The challenged party having the selection of weapons and ground, Capt. Shaughnessy chose navy pistols at ten paces, and named the Louisiana shore near by as the place of combat, and thither, in company with two or three friends and a surgeon, he at once repaired. After having waited for many hours in vain for the appearance of the belligerent newspaper disciple, it was ascertained that Wright, for some reason, had lingered in Vicksburg until arrested and placed under bond to keep the peace. Hearing of this little act of diplomacy, Shaughnessy's friends returned to the city, and, without delay, put a check for the amount of Wright's recognizance at the disposal of his bondsmen, thus setting him at liberty to fight or "back down" entirely, as the case might be. Some thirty-six hours beyond the time for the hostile meeting had passed when the *Herald* chieftain, in suitable war-paint, accompanied by his friends, appeared upon the scene. On their arrival the thick gloom of a foggy night on the Mississippi set in, and it was thought by the party last on the grounds that the darkness would preclude the possibility of a passage at arms until daylight. Capt. Shaughnessy's friends objected to another postponement on any pretext whatever, contending that fires could be built, from the light of which a collision, as fair at least for one as the other, could be had. While the communications incident to all this were passing and repassing, a proposition for the settlement of the difficulty came from Wright's seconds. This was finally agreed upon, Wright first withdrawing the charges made by him through his paper, reflecting upon Shaughnessy, when the latter, in turn, recalled the offensive language applied to Wright.

Thus the family were left alone, and without the hope of aid; menaced and threatened on every hand by the barbarians who surrounded them, thirsting for the little blood that remained. The few friends who had come to their aid were ready to do and die, if necessary, but utterly powerless should the threatened attack be made.

Is it to be wondered at, then, that we are now called upon to record the worst?

The following private letter, addressed by Mrs. Chisolm to Capt. Shaughnessy, but a few days after his leaving for Jackson, explains itself and shows something of her feelings on the receipt of the intelligence that the Governor had expressed his inability or unwillingness to assist her:

DeKalb, Miss., May 9th, '77.

Capt. M. Shaughnessy:

Kind Friend of my Husband:—I was both grieved and surprised to learn through this afternoon's mail, from Gov. Stone's Private Secretary, that the Governor refused us any protection other than that of F. C. Sinclair, who, with the pretense of an arrest, played into the hands of the mob. Having great reliance in your judgment, will, and fearless bravery, I hasten to communicate the fact to you. I hear nothing tending to give me quiet, and everything to the reverse. Both husband and daughter are suffering severely, more so than when you were here.

Hoping to hear from you, or better, see you,

I am very respectfully and gratefully,

Emily S. M. Chisolm.

One day, not far from this time, the writer was sitting by the bed-side holding Judge Chisolm's hand, when he gave the grip of a Master Mason. Thinking that he desired to communicate something, I said:

"Judge, I did not remember that you were a Mason!"

"Yes," replied he, "I *was* a Mason, but the men who tried to murder me and my children the other day, for a long time undertook to force me to renounce my republicanism and join them in their nefarious political schemes.

To accomplish this they threatened to expel me from the lodge. Failing in that, they sought to blacken my character in every possible way, and finally expelled me; but even after that I was told by Gully, T. S. Murphy, and Charles Bell, all prominent members of the lodge, if I would only *keep quiet,* politically, that I would again be restored to honorable membership."

This is only one of the many affecting incidents which occurred during the dark hours preceding the final scene of desolation and woe, in witnessing which the stoutest heart must have sunk.

Two weeks of anxious watching and labor by day and night, with varying shadows of hope and fear on the part of family and friends, passed by, while the pain and suffering of the victims steadily increased, until Sunday evening, just before eight o'clock of May 13th, Judge Chisolm died, with his head resting in the arms of his devoted wife. By advice of the surgeon, a knowledge of his death was carefully kept from Cornelia. To do this, we were compelled, almost by force, to carry the widowed mother into another portion of the house, where her screams could not be heard by the suffering girl. During the terrible night which followed—terrible indeed to the inmates of that household—Cornelia, many times called for her "mamma," who was then wholly unable to come to her. The poor girl was deceived with the story that her mother had a very severe head-ache and had lain down for a little rest, and the doctor's orders were that she must not be disturbed. In this way, Cornelia was pacified until the morning came, when she again called for her, and would hardly consent to be put off longer. "Only think," she said, "I have not seen mamma since last night, before dark; now you must let her come to me!"

After having been informed of Cornelia's request to see her, I asked Mrs. Chisolm if she could go into her presence without betraying any unusual emotion, calculated to arouse a suspicion in Cornelia's mind of the death of her father. "Yes," said she, "I am equal to anything;" and, after bathing her face in cold water, she walked deliberately into the room and caressed the fatherless girl, who lay there unconscious of her orphanage. That morning the coffin came and Judge Chisolm's body was carried off and buried as Johnny's had been, two weeks before.

Tuesday, the 15th, the physician came in and informed the writer (who at the time was her only attendant) of his determination to perform an operation on Cornelia's arm, which had become very much swollen and inflamed from erysipelas and other causes, some of the wounds having but imperfect drainage. A similar operation, though not so severe, had been tried before with very satisfactory results, and the doctor's opinion was that this done she would begin to recover at once. The necessary preparations for this operation were entered upon with the greatest reluctance, as the girl was very much reduced, and more especially as chloroform had to be administered. This, however, was given only in small quantities, enough to deaden the sensibilities, though not sufficient to put her entirely under its influence.

The surgeon lanced the arm in several places, the blood flowing profusely but before the operation had been completed she returned to consciousness, complained of great pain and immediately fainted. All needful restoratives were at hand, and from this she was soon rallied, but fainted again, exclaiming as the swoon came upon her, " O ! how dark, dark, dark ! Will the light never come again ?" Only that light which illumines the pathway of the glorified in heaven, appeared to her again.

Every remedy was applied that could possibly be devised, but she continued to sink. The day was bright and balmy, and as the breath of the dying girl grew short and labored, the doors and windows were opened and the fragrance of sweet flowers, from a hundred different varieties growing in the yard, wafted by a gentle and refreshing breeze, filled the room. A pure white lily, almost the last object upon which she bestowed a look or caress, rested on her bosom as she lay in a reclining posture in a large arm chair. But the scent of her favorite roses, or the touch of soft winds from the cool forest shade failed to catch that eye already dimmed by the leaden shades of death. The heart-broken mother and little brothers, wild with grief, gathered round, and their cries and sobs went out over the frowning walls of the county jail, and far beyond the limits of that blood-cursed town.

"O ! God of mercy," cried Clay, " must sister die, too ? My sweet, sweet sister ! Murdered ! murdered ! murdered !" The stricken family, together with the few friends that stood by, sank upon the floor by the martyr's side, while in the mute eloquence of woe, all prayed God to spare her precious life. As long as respiration lasted her clear and powerful intellect seemed to be at work, for, in answer to the appeals of her mother to "*try* to breathe again for papa's sake," she would struggle for another breath; but already her spirit was reaching out to be welcomed by that of her beloved father in another world; and " Homeward she walked with God's benediction upon her."

Among the stricken mourners gathered there, none were more deeply moved than the negroes about the place, many of whom had watched the growth of this bright being from a child, and who loved her with an honest and unselfish devotion. These gathered in large numbers as they had done at the death-bed of Judge Chisolm, and their tears were mingled with those of the family and friends.

At two o'clock her spirit took its flight; and there, almost under the shadow of the slaughter-pen, where the victims were offered up, its grim walls looking down as fixed and immovable as the hearts of those whose savage thirst for blood had thus been satiated, lay the mangled corpse of this pure and innocent girl, with the dark blue marks left by blows from the assassin's hand still visible upon her fair face and brow, now calmly composed in death.

The loving hands of Mrs. Griffin, Mrs. Hopper, Mrs. Rush and Miss McDevitt, dressed and prepared her for the grave, and if an angel from heaven had lain there asleep, its loveliness would have been eclipsed by the surpassing beauty of that dead girl.

By the direction of the physician, the mother, who now sat cold and dumb and tearless, was placed under the closest surveillance, as it was feared by all that she would become hopelessly insane.

Wednesday the coffin came, and the martyred remains followed those of the father and brother a distance of twenty-two miles through a desolate and unreclaimed region, right past the haunts of the men whose hands were yet dripping with her blood, and who stood by the roadside and gazed upon the mournful scene with an expression of stolid indifference. From early morning until five o'clock in the evening the solemn march proceeded, when a bright and cheerful little spot broke upon the view — an oasis in the great desert of Kemper County — the place where our heroine was born nineteen years before, and where now the father, daughter and son sleep side by side.

Thus, within sight of three christian churches, one after another the victims sank and died, and not a minister of the gospel nor a member of the congregation with which the mother and murdered daughter worshiped, ever offered to cross the threshold of the house of mourning. One after another the mangled forms were carried out and buried, with just enough hands to perform the manual labor incident thereto, and not a requiem was sung nor a benediction offered, save only the prayers which came silently and spontaneously from the hearts of the faithful few who stood around.

After diligent inquiry, it is yet to be learned that any clergyman preaching in DeKalb, Scooba or Meridian — all immediately adjoining towns — has publicly alluded to this in any way. What may be said of a condition of society, which so bridles the mouths of the chosen messengers of the Great Prince of Peace, that they dare not lift their voices against such a crime as this; and that because of the peculiar political faith of those who are made victims of the sacrifice?

Thus the curtain falls upon this act in the tragedy, and with it ends the career of a family whose only rule of law in the domestic circle was that of love, and whose worst offense against their fellows, was the free exercise of an honest conviction which the constitution of the country guarantees to its humblest citizen. From the father down, a kiss or a fond caress was the only sure password to their hearts, and the only punishment ever offered for any disobedience of parental authority or other supposed wrong-doing.

Cornelia, at once a martyr to a God-like filial affection, and a victim of savage outlawry, the oldest of the children and the brightest jewel of the household, was the star of her mother's hope, and her father's especial pet and idol. Happy and vivacious, tender, true and faithful to every kindly impulse, her heart was capable of loving the whole world. Possessed of superior intelligence, her character was graced with a purity which gave her an elevated and commanding place in the scale of young and useful womanhood, into which she had just entered, and her untimely and terrible death has left a wound in the hearts of all who knew her well which time can never heal, while a million accursed lives like that of Rosser and his followers can never atone for a single drop of her pure and innocent blood.

CHAPTER XXI.

The traces of the bloody sacrifice extended around the iron cages from the top of the jail all along the staircase and hall way to the outside entrance; over the smooth, grassy common to the house; through the little window from the back porch and across the floor to the room where the wounded were placed; and from there to every closet and corner where busy fingers, leaving red stains, turned in search of lint, bandages or whatever could be found for the relief or comfort of the wounded. These crimson marks had scarcely had time to dry when every species of falsification and evasion of or detraction from the real facts concerning the massacre were put forth, through the agency of the local press and voluntary newspaper writers of the State. A number of journals, it is true, condemned the crime as the murderers themselves should have been condemned and executed long ago; and among the people there was a goodly number who really sympathized with the family and their friends; but these were slow and exceedingly cautious in the manifestations of their feelings. A communication of the kind alluded to, which appeared in one of the leading newspapers, is here given. It tacitly admits the horrors of the slaughter in an endeavor to find justification for the act. The assertions made by "A Subscriber" have been fully discussed and answered in the preceding pages, and this sweeping and unqualified statement of an individual who was himself one of the prime movers in the conspiracy, is not nor can it be sustained by a single corroborating circumstance, or witness, living or dead. It is reproduced to show the spirit which moves the hearts of these men, after the voices of their victims have been silenced forever, and they seek to violate the graves filled by their own red hands, when no power on earth remains to vindicate the honor of the dead. Here is the letter:

DeKalb, Miss., June 15, 1877.

Editor Meridian Mercury:

Knowing that you are using all your powers to put the Kemper riot in its true light before the world, I have concluded to give you a few of the leading facts in respect to it. During the last eight or nine years, Kemper county has been infested with a set of well organized forgers, thieves, robbers and murderers. The very best man among them was without a peer in villainy among the Murrell or Copelan clans. They would rob, forge and steal by day, and kill and murder by night. For illustration: Numbers of men, and women too, widows, have paid their taxes every year on their lands and have their receipts to prove it; but their lands have gone to the State for from five to eight years, and are delinquent and not one cent of taxes paid in. Men who now, under honest tax gatherers, pay eight to ten dollars, under the Chisolm-Gilmer clan paid from twenty-eight to thirty-five dollars; the twenty to twenty-five dollars was clear robbery of the people every year. They perpetrated frauds and swindles innumerable, mostly in county warrants, some of which I could specify if time and space would allow. The first of the bloody crimes was the murder of J. H. Ball in 1869. It was peculiarly atrocious and heart-rending. His house was surrounded at night with himself and family in it. Guns were fired into it, and the vigorous assault demonstrated the murderous intent. It was death to remain, and almost certain death to fly. The latter presented a gleam of hope and he tried it. He cleared the house and passed his assailants, but was seen, pursued and barbarously butchered away out in his cotton field. He did not die immediately, but lived to tell who his immediate murderers were. They were negroes known to be tools of Chisolm. That, with a thrilling scene between him and Chisolm about three weeks before, with no eye to see and no ear to hear, when and where it was in truth Ball sacrificed his own life to his weak humanity, demonstrates, to a moral certainty, that his killing was of Chisolm's procuring. He was shot and killed in the night time, if not, to quote the special correspondent of the New York *Tribune* "by some one in hiding by the road side." The proofs were produced in this case, but the parties were acquitted. It was only a white man and a democrat was killed. In 1870, Sam Gully was killed by Ben Rush, on the streets of DeKalb. He was tried and acquitted, though he had deliberately gone out with his gun. to intercept his victim with intention to commit murder. Hal Dawson was killed, in 1871, by Bill Davis, at Scooba, in conspiracy with J. P. Gilmer, two notorious members of the Chisolm clan. Gilmer inveigled him to where Davis could shoot him down with impunity, and shot two bullets into his head after he was down. Chisolm was all-powerful then, and as sheriff protected the murderers, and so powerful was he in his wickedness that they were not only never punished, but never in any danger of being punished by any legal method. On the contrary, he was rewarded by being elected to a seat in the State Senate; and ever after that was near to Chisolm and a co-worker in all his schemes. The virtuous friendship of Damon and Pythias, long ago, was not surpassed by the love and affection these twin workers of iniquity bore each other. W. S. Gambrel, a mild republican, and generally beliked by the good white people, was State Senator when Hal Dawson was killed and Gilmer set his covetous eyes upon the office as a reward for bloody service. It was easy for them to do, and poor Gambrel " was shot by some person in hiding by the road side," and thus was made the vacancy in the State Senate for Gilmer to fill as his reward for killing Hal Dawson. In killing Gambrel they accomplished two desirable ends — they got rid of a man who refused to become an accomplice in their villainies, and made the way clear to reward a favorite.

A young man by the name of Floyd was killed in his store, in 1873, by a hired assassin. The murderer was arrested, but Chisolm was sheriff and permitted him to escape. The murderer rode away a gray pony furnished by McClellan, the "British subject." He took up and staid awhile in Jasper County, and in a drunken spree told the tale, and then left for parts unknown. About this time, Bob Dabbs was waylaid in DeKalb, and shot and killed by a negro clansman. There was then an unsuccessful attempt to assassinate Mr. Thomas Morton " by some person in hiding by the road side," occurred in 1875. A charge of buckshot was sent through his shoulder, severely wounding him. Dennis Jones, colored, was shot and killed " by some person in hiding by the road side," in 1876. The shooting of John W. Gully in December last, had the design of it been fully successful, would have been the best laid plan of them all. He was to have been killed on the road between two negro houses, one hundred and fifty to two hundred yards apart, and it was to have been laid on them. And on his final taking off in April, it was attempted to make the same impression that it was the deed of negroes, by robbing him of his boots, hat, pistols and money. Chisolm had made a threat that he intended to make the people of the county feel him. From his past record and present success in procuring a good citizen to be killed, the people might well dread he would make good the threat, and enquire, who next? That question presented a horrible and maddening thought. For ten years Chisolm and his gang had pursued their course of public robbery and private murder, unchecked and unbaffled by human laws, and they had begun, now, to execute his latest threat, to make the people of the county feel him in a bloody murder, and the dread question each man who helped to bury John W. Gully put to himself—who next? What wonder the next day brought the DeKalb riot? The 29th of April tells the tale of people in madness thwarting the bloody threat in blood. Put forward, as it has been done, in its worst aspect, we must confess that the killing of the son and daughter looks savage-like; but stated in its true light and without any coloring, and it is not so bad. The guards stationed in the jail all agree, that after the first gun fired by Chisolm, which killed Dr. Rosser, several shots were fired at him filling the room with smoke. The little boy, frightened, ran in front of his father, and he, seeing him indistinctly, supposed him to be one of his assailants, and shot him. His daughter was wounded, frantically clinging to her father by some one over excited and rendered incautious thereby. It was deplorable, and none deplore it as the actors in the tragedy. These men, whom no written law could ever reach, the unwritten higher law took hold on that 29th of April; its adjudications were soon made, and the execution of them a terrible example, for the crime which has had a long and successful career, defying law or evading it by ways scarcely less criminal than the infraction of the law whose penalties they avoid.

A Subscriber.

The men against whom the grave charges in the
above are aimed cannot answer them. They are dead.
They cannot compel the murderer to produce the testimony against them, or by his failure to do so prove himself a liar as well. The falsifier and traducer believes he
has now as little to fear from resistance to the assaults
of his envenomed tongue, as the assassin did from
defense against his bullets after the chosen victims had
been disarmed and securely fastened in jail. But in this
at least let us hope they have committed an error.
There is but one statement in this voluntary libel having
the semblance of truth, and that is found in the paragraph relating to the existence, in Kemper county, of a
" well organized band of forgers, thieves, robbers and
murderers; the very best man among them being without a peer in villainy among the Murrell or Copeland
clans." If the writer had gone back forty years instead
of "eight," in dating the beginning of organized robbery
and murder in Kemper county, his communication would
have been spared the condemnation of unblushing and
unqualified falsehood; for Copeland himself, in his "Confession on the Gallows," as published by Dr. F. R. S.
Pitts, the sheriff who executed him, draws heavily from
Kemper county for the material of which that thrilling
and blood-curdling story of crime and outlawry is composed. The names of some of these men are there
given. Their descendants are living in Kemper and
adjoining counties to-day, and the most diabolical murders and robberies of which the annals of crime furnish
proof have been committed within its borders during the

past six months, and there never has been but one white man executed in the county for any offense since the admission of the State into the Union.

The question is now asked, if the charges of the writer quoted be true, why were these "great criminals" — Chisolm, Gilmer and others — never punished, or sought to be punished, in some legal way, after the overthrow of their power and the corrupt rule of 'radicalism' in the county?" Rush had gone from their reach into another State, it is true; though nothing but the fear of death from a concealed foe caused his flight. The two Hoppers and Rosenbaum, all of them "accessory to the killing of Gully," and thieves and robbers on the most gigantic scale — "the good people" of Kemper would have us believe — are alive and well to-day, and two of them are still within the county, and they fear nothing but the murderous bullet from ambush. No process of the law has any terror for them. Rosenbaum and one of the Hoppers, under the threat of assassination, have been forced to seek employment elsewhere, and the other Hopper has been whipped into temporary obedience to the will of the Klan; other than this they are in no danger. If Judge Chisolm, as sheriff, ever "robbed the widow and the orphan," as claimed, why were not the "tax receipts" in the possession of those robbed produced in court, the sheriff sued upon his bond for misdemeanor in office, the money recovered and himself sent to the penitentiary?

But as an ultimatum and a proof positive of his many crimes, the argument is made that Judge Chisolm grew rich while sheriff. It is true, as stated before, that he accumulated property while in that office, as did every other sheriff in the State during a corresponding period, without regard to party affiliations. The position is admitted to be the most lucrative, as it is certainly the most influential in the disposition and control of public patronage within the State. This, no doubt, is the secret of the great crime, growing out of its possession for so many years by some one adverse to the Gullys and their especial favorites.

But the groans of the wounded, pent up by barred windows and closed blinds, were yet wringing the hearts of the few friends and relatives on watch, while editorials like the following were being printed and circulated throughout the country.

The Meridian *Mercury*, always first in a good work, regaled its peaceful and law-loving readers with sentiments of this kind:

Perhaps the time is now ripe for us to speak what we had intended to.

What Governor Stone has requested Judge Hamm to do about holding a special term for an early investigation we don't know. Judge Hamm has ordered no special term, and we think it is safe to predict that he will not. If we ever had a strong conviction about anything, we never had a stronger one than that it is best not.

April 29th, in DeKalb, never ought to be investigated, and if wisdom and statemanship prevail, never will be. On that day, the higher law, which antedates common law and all other law, ousted them all and their ministers of jurisdiction, and for a brief period of time, sufficient to its purposes, held sway. Its judgments were final.

As they affect the living and the dead, they are *res adjudicata,* and will ever remain so. No court is competent to disturb them. Every attempt to review them will be both futile and mischievous. Special instructions to grand jurors are likely to go unheeded, and *to save an exhibition of their impotency* had best not be given. The best thing the law and the ministers can do about the tragedy is to save their strength for the future as wiser than wasting it foolishly and vainly on the past.

*   *   *   *   *   *   *

From all accounts, we estimate there were three to four hundred men. Every man of these was equally a principal in the murder, if murder was committed, with any other man. *Besides this, nearly every adult white man in the county, who was not present, is resolved to stand by those who were there, and approve them as good and true citizens and not criminals.* Can three or four hundred men who were present, and all principals alike in any crime committed, with an entire county besides resolved to protect them against any consequences the law denounces against their acts, be indicted, tried, convicted and hung or sent to the penitentiary for life?

This was followed by Mr. P. K. Mayers, of the Handsboro *Democrat,* who murdered Mr. Orr at Pass Christian, in open day, and now writes editorials complimenting the courage and chivalry of his Kemper brethren, who, if possible, are more cowardly and brutal than himself.

Here is the language of the *Democrat :*

We have refrained from editorial comment upon the unfortunate but necessary killing of scallawag Gilmer, and the wounding of scallawag ex-Judge Chisolm, in Kemper County, because we were loth to blame before we were in possession of all the facts, and because we were determined not to justify a lawless act, no matter by whom committed. We are for compelling individuals to seek remedies for wrongs, real or supposed, in such a way as not to endanger the peace of society. But when the conduct of individuals offending is so violent, that society must be outraged and ruined before legal remedies can be applied, the summary punishment of such individuals becomes pardonable.

The facts in the case under discussion, disclose a fearful state of affairs in Kemper County. It appears that Gilmer, Chisolm and their confederates, for several years pursued a system of robbing, murder and assassination, and have defied and eluded the law. Three times they attempted to murder the unfortunate man, whose untimely death led speedily to retributive justice on their own heads. The last time they succeeded. It appears that the barbarous brutes and cowards, in addition to the waylaying and butchering of two Gullys, have stolen the records of the Courts, and thus cut off the only chance society had to protect itself. What wonder is it, then, that the people outraged have at last seized the law in their own hands, and administered a fierce and swift justice on the heads of the butchers of the respected but unfortunate Gullys. However we may deplore the manner of their "taking off," we cannot but be glad society is rid of the monsters Gilmer & Co.

We regret to observe, on the part of all the Radical press of the State, a disposition to make political capital out of the unhappy affair, and we are ashamed of that portion of the Democratic press, which has been swift to condemn the avengers of the Gullys, simply because surviving scallawags and carpet-baggers of no better repute than their defunct co-partners in crime may howl over their timely demise. Doubtless these wretches, like their Mormon prototypes, Brigham Young and "Mountain Meadow" Lee, would even be glad at society patiently bearing their atrocities. It will not do so. They must meet the consequences of their crimes. For years they have plundered, robbed, murdered, burned and assassinated with impunity. They must now pay with their lives and necks for a continuance of these acts. The slow but leaden hand of Justice crushed the Mollie Maguires of Pennsylvania, it will crush the banded clan of murdering scallawags and carpet-baggers in Mississippi. We are for law where it can be had, but above all for justice.

The Jackson *Clarion,* which is really an able and influential journal, and truthfully represents the brain and heart of Mississippi's best citizenship, comments upon this grave affair as follows:

Major Ethel Barksdale is responsible for this:

The long era of corrupt and inefficient government, through which both Mississippi and Louisiana have passed, has brought about a want of confidence in and respect for the law, and given to violent and lawless men a dangerous latitude of action. This evil must be vigorously eradicated from both States. We have heard of no more atrocious crime, than that which was perpetrated in Kemper County, and Gov. Stone has now an opportunity, by fearless and determined action, to strike such terror to the hearts of lawless men in Mississippi, that he will, if he avails himself of it, have little trouble of a similar nature in the future." — *New Orleans Democrat.*

This is a specimen of the tub, which some Southern newspapers that ought to know better, is throwing out to the Northern whale, which they imagine is craving for a sensational feast. The conductors of those papers cannot but know, that sometimes there are evils to be uprooted, for which no peaceable methods provide sufficient remedies, and that others besides "violent and

lawless men" resort to them. Chief among them is sys-
tematic and premeditated assassination, the evidence of
which is necessarily circumstantial, but of which there is,
nevertheless, confirmation as strong as proof of holy
writ to the public mind. That the Kemper County
affair is the product of the bad passions which were
propagated under Radical misrule, and that they were
indulged by depraved and vicious men, who flourished
under it, cannot be questioned. But that the men who,
to rid the community of the evils which it "inflicted were
compelled to resort to summary measures were "lawless
and violent" in the sense employed, we utterly deny.

If our New Orleans cotemporary will tax his memory
just a little he will readily recall " crimes " equally as
" atrocious " as the Kemper affair, when outraged communities were forced, by abuses for which they were not
responsible, to inflict summary. vengeance upon evil
doers. It happened at Mechanics' Institute, in New
Orleans, in 1868; in Grant parish in 1874; in New
Orleans again on the memorable 14th of September;
at Clinton, Miss., in 1875, and at Hamburg, South Caro-
lina, in 1876. If our New Orleans neighbor will tax his
memory he will recall the scenes at San Francisco just a
few years preceding the war; and the summary vengeance the Indiana people inflicted upon the Reno clan,
after finding that the slow processes of the law were
wholly inadequate to the punishment of assassins who
lurked in thickets on the way-side, and made their tracks
under the cover of darkness.

*　　*　　*　　*　　*　　*　　*

We don't understand what is meant by the call upon
Governor Stone to strike " terror into the hearts of lawless men in Mississippi." The governor is as much
bound by the law as other people are, and it distinctly
prescribes his duties. It gives him no authority to try

anybody, to hang anybody, or to put anybody in the penitentiary. The men engaged in the Kemper affair did their work in open day. They will not run away nor hide themselves. They are amenable to the laws, and judicial tribunals are established to try them. It will be time enough for the governor to exercise his power as commander-in-chief when the laws for the punishment of the accused are defied and the courts are shown to be powerless to execute their decrees.

The Okalona *Southern States* thus addresses the people of the North, whose eyes are turned upon Mississippi in just and withering condemnation of its whole people for suffering such acts as are here recorded to go unheeded and unwhipped:

Talk of the Kemper county outrage! Was that anything when compared to the murders, and burning, and devilish outrages of every character and description that you visited upon us while the civil war was in progress? Down, down on your knees you wretches, and pray God to forgive your atrocities before you dare to rebuke us for anything. We have had just about enough of this tigerish interference on your part.

Elsewhere, mention is made of the responsibility of Thomas S. Gathright in bringing about the horrors of the 29th of April, in DeKalb, and here again an opportunity is found for quoting his language bearing upon that matter. What is reproduced will be found in a letter written by Mr. Gathright to the Jackson *Clarion*, and bears date, "Central Texas, June 1, 1877." It is over the well known *nom de plume* of "William." Here is his language:

It is high time that some people in Mississippi were

learning the lesson written in Kemper in lines of blood, that the tyrant, the traitor and the assassin will sooner or later be overtaken by a frightful retribution, and that all who are partisans and mourners of such are but biding their time.

CHAPTER XXII.

Time advances, and while these scenes are fresh in the memory of all who witnessed them, five victims offered as a bloody sacrifice, and three others are driven from their families and homes, it transpires that the pretended evidence of their guilt is no where to be found. Not even a resort to the halter or lash could wring from the two negroes a statement calculated to imperil the life of an innocent man. The witnesses whose names appeared on the forged warrant of arrest, have been questioned and declare their entire ignorance of the facts, if such facts ever had an existence save in the fertile brain of the perjurer and assassin. The next startling intelligence comes from the same reliable source quoted in the preceding chapter—the Meridian *Mercury*—with an admission like the following:

We have information of a fact which, if true, as we believe it to be, leads almost irresistibly to the conclusion that Chisolm was an accomplice of the assassin of Gully.

Ah! we are now consoled with a declaration from the executioner that he is in hopes, ere long, to be able to fasten the evidence of guilt upon those whose heads have already fallen into the basket. The Vicksburg *Herald* comes to the defense of the *Mercury* and, in a similar strain, says:

It is now coming to light that there is some very convincing proof that Gilmer, Chisolm and Company were accessory to the cowardly murder of John W. Guily.

Following this, the paper first named again steps to the front and places the question beyond the reach of a doubt:

We have stated the "fact" for "information of the *Times*," which "leads almost irresistibly to the conclusion that Chisolm was an accomplice in the assassination of Gully." Though Rush was unseen to the general public after the attempt of the 20th of December, he was seen in Chisolm's house — business house — in DeKalb, with some of the Chisolm gang, in the night time. Even in that secret place, he kept his double-barrel gun in hand. He went behind the counter to mix him a drink of whisky, and yet held on to his gun the while. This is a bit of circumstantial evidence, it is true, but we ask the *Times* if it does not "lead almost irresistibly to the conclusion that Chisolm was an accomplice."

All that the author of the above seems to require is a little time. If the people will remain silent and allow the ghosts of the murdered father and children to rest quietly in their graves, sufficient proof *will* be found to convince the world that Cornelia and Johnny, McLellan and Gilmer and Judge Chisolm ought to have been entrapped in jail by the sheriff and there butchered.

Whether in compliance with this prophetic advice or not, those entrusted with the execution of the law have rested quietly enough, God knows.

A few short and eventful weeks have followed, while the hearts of the widow and orphan, still writhing under

their bereavement, and pouring forth a ceaseless fountain
of tears, have anxiously waited the fulfillment of the
above revelation, terrible though its realization might be
to them, having nothing better offered upon which to
settle down and rest a future of absolute hopelessness
and despair. While thus living in daily anticipation of
this promised disclosure, another and a very different
scene suddenly bursts upon the view, and which estab-
lishes conclusively and at once the entire innocence of
the accused, and as quickly and effectually exposes the
enormities of the conspiracy, through means of which
the "Slaughter of the Innocents" was procured. Reference is had to the affidavit sent by B. F. Rush, from
Russellville, Arkansas, which clearly shows the fact that
he could not possibly have had anything to do with the
assassination of Gully on the 26th of April, as he was
at Russellville on that very day. The affidavit is here
presented, bearing the signatures of twenty-five good
citizens of that place:

THE STATE OF ARKANSAS, }
Pope County. }

To all whom it may concern :
We, the undersigned, citizens of said county and
State, hereby certify that we are acquainted with B. F.
Rush, and have been since some time in March last. He
has been in regular attendance at our Sabbath school;
he is now living and has been since the time above
specified, with one J. W. Harkey, which fact many of us
know of our own personal knowledge, having been at
said Harkey's, and meeting with said Rush there, and
well know that he was not nor could have been in Mississippi at the time he was alleged to have been. In

testimony whereof, we hereunto affix our names this the
10th day of June, A.D. 1877:

C. B. FALKINGTON,   M. W. PARKER,
L. G. TURNER,   WM. DUNCAN,
J. M. MOORE,   W. H. RUSHING,
J. J. STOUT,   G. W. RUSHING,
JOHN L. STEVENSON,   W. M. MULLINS,
B. A. TULLY,   O. D. WILSON,
E. B. WOOTEN,   S. J. MULLINS,
W. J. BRIMAN,   DAVID McCORMICK,
H. C. HAMILTON,   A. B. WILLIFSON,
L. D. BRYANT,   J. S. WHEELER,
J. M. BERRYHILL,   Z. T. TURNER,
A. P. BRYANT,   A. H. HUMPHREYS.

THE STATE OF ARKANSAS, }
   County of Pope. }

I, J. W. Sharkey, do solemnly swear that I am well
acquainted with B. F. Rush, and have been since the
22d day of March, 1877, since which time he has continuously lived with me, and I know that he was at work
with me at my farm, in said county, on the 26th day of
April, 1877.   J. W. SHARKEY.

Sworn to and subscribed before me this 13th day of
June 1877, and I certify that said affiant is a creditable
and respectable citizen of said county.

      A. J. BAYLISS,
[Seal.] Clerk Circuit Court Pope Co., Ark.

But not yet satisfied, an effort is made to bring Rush
from Arkansas on a requisition, charging him with the
intent to kill Gully on the 20th of December, at the
time the latter was wounded. That everybody believed
if Rush was brought back he would be murdered there

is no doubt, and that Governor Stone himself entertained this view is shown by the fact that, after reflection, he telegraphed the governor of Arkansas — Mr.
Miller — not to recognize the requisition. Upon this
despatch of Governor Stone the prisoner, after having
been arrested and placed in the hands of the agent for
Mississippi — a member of the Gully family—was released
on an imperative order from Governor Miller, of Arkansas.

The following letter, written by Rush a few days
later, will explain the matter more fully, and shows the
extent of this conspiracy to take his life:

RUSSELLVILLE, ARK., July 1, 1877.
Dear Friend: Enclosed I send you a copy of a letter which I have written Gov. Stone, of Mississippi, in
reference to my recent arrest, in which you will see that
I have been kidnapped and put to a great deal of
trouble; though, thank God, I had the sympathy of all
Russellville and vicinity, and I state to you in confidence,
Gully would never have gotten away from Russellville
with me, from what I have since learned. My friends
were on the alert. I am fully pursuaded that it was a
grand conspiracy for my assassination. I don't believe
I would have been permitted to have seen Little Rock.
I am confident, and so are my friends, that the plan was
to kill me before reaching Mississippi, for it appears that
Gully would not release me under any consideration, but
said I would be released in Little Rock. After the
Governor had ordered my release, he then refused to
allow me the privilege of a private conference with my
attorneys, saying that he was governed by what his
brother-in-law, Col. Jacaway, advised. The sheriff, after
seeing Gov. Stone's despatch, which virtually released
me, when I asked him, as my protector, not to deliver
me into the hands of my enemies, did so, and then pro-

ceeded to take from my pocket my key, and dive into my private letters and matters generally. Hand-cuffed they took me to the hotel, where, thank God, I had good friends, Gully not being acquainted. I was lodged in a room up stairs, and there, by Gully, *chained down.* You can well imagine my feelings. The landlord, Mr. Tucker, gave up his room below, and occupied one adjoining mine. He slept none, I am confident, because I could hear him at all hours. I will ever bear him in kind remembrance. Judge Davis, Col. Wood and W. C. Ford were my attorneys. My financial matters were limited, but with the aid and assistance of kind friends — Mr. J. W. Haskey especially — I was furnished with a plenty to put me through. I looked upon my situation as a life and death matter, and so did my friends. You can have my letter to Gov. Stone published, if you think best. I would like my friends abroad to know of my troubles. I have now made up my mind to go to some Northern city. It appears that I am to be persecuted and hounded down all my life. I am in a critical condition. My friends think it best for me to keep private, not knowing who may be lurking for me. I am now out on the mountain writing. Am out of money, and in my condition, can make none. My friends think I had best not be stirring about. Would like for you to go up to DeKalb, at your earliest convenience. and read this letter to my wife and children.

Your friend,   B. F. RUSH.

P. S.— If my friends in Mississippi see proper to help me — I do not ask it as a gift — I am yet able, notwithstanding I am shot up and crippled for life, to make a living, and more, too, and will repay all they may contribute to my relief in this time of trouble.

B. F. R.

With the affidavit presented by Rush, the bottom upon which the superstructure of the conspiracy was reared, falls out. To find palliation or justification now, the conspirator must go outside of the assassination of Gully, and beyond the reach of any record left by the men upon whose heads have already fallen the visitations of his deep villainy. Rush, having been in Arkansas continuously from the first of March preceding, could not have killed Gully on the 26th of April, at DeKalb, Mississippi. This, to the friends of the martyred dead, signifies much, as it places beyond the possibility of belief the last charge which their persecutors have been able to bring against them. Yet, to the red-handed plotters of iniquity, it all goes for naught, as their work is accomplished, and they are left free to commit any similar act whenever occasion presents.

But a sense of shame seems to have found lodgement in the hearts of some of the apologists for the killing of defenseless women and children, and sooner than maintain absolute silence, the following grave and alarming aspersion is cast upon the physician under whose treatment the wounded sank and died. If Mississippians are content with the assertion and belief that a surgeon, because of his blind adherence to the peculiar political faith which they have made essential to citizenship, would suffer the victims of prejudice and hate to die when it was within the power of human skill to have saved them, after having been entrusted to his sacred care as a physician, then indeed the case becomes "tenfold" more horrifying. In connection with this subject, the Vicksburg *Herald* comes to the relief of the broken-hearted survivors, even at the risk of the terrible consequences foreshadowed above, in language as follows:

The accident of Miss Chisolm's death caused by malpractice, and not by her slight wound, adds tenfold to the deplorable consequences.

Now that the "good people" of Kemper have had ample opportunity to assert their inherent manhood in the selection of leaders whose "virtue and intelligence" is found to be in keeping with that of the sovereigns themselves, and when again it is asked why these men never were convicted of the multifarious crimes with which they were and are still so freely charged, it is said that the courts and the juries were so completety under their control as to make the indictment of one of their political faith an impossibility. Let us examine into the facts, and see if this be true or false.

Since 1866, the boards of supervisors elected in the county, with the bare exception of the year 1869, have been under the management of the democratic party. That is to say: a majority of each board has been conservative and democratic, which signifies its entire control by that party. To make this statement good, and place the fact beyond contradiction, the names of the men comprising the various boards in the order of their election, since the year 1866 is given, designating each by showing opposite the name their political affiliation:

BOARD OF 1866.

John R. Brittain,	Democrat.
R. Jarvis,	"
D. H. Garner,	"
C. F. Johnson,	————
James W. Hardin,	Democrat.

BOARD OF 1867.

John H. Oden, ...	Democrat.
J. W. Hardin, ...	"
M. D. Crawford, ...	"
R. Jarvis, ...	"
C. F. Johnson, ...	————

BOARD OF 1869.

T. N. Bethany, ...	Republican.
D. McNeil, ...	"
G. E. Priddy, ...	Independent.
Wm. Ezell, ...	Republican.
Hozie Flore, ...	————

BOARD OF 1871.

E. Edwards, ...	Democrat.
D. McNeil, ...	Republican.
Wm. Hudson, ...	Democrat.
G. E. Priddy, ...	Independent.
T. N. Bethany, ...	Republican.

BOARD OF 1872.

Moses Halford, ...	Republican.
John R. Davis, ...	Democrat.
R. Nave, ...	Republican.
G. E. Priddy, ...	Independent
W. K. Stennis, ...	Democrat.

BOARD OF 1874.

John R. Davis, ...	Democrat.
E. Edwards, ...	"
J. A. Jenkins, ...	"
R. Nave, ...	Republican.
T. W. Adams, ...	"

BOARD OF 1876.

T. H. Hampton, ...	Democrat.
John R. Davis, ...	"
E. Edwards, ...	"
J. C. Carpender, ...	"
Robert Griggs, ...	Republican.

Following this the Revised Code of Mississippi is quoted, showing the power that a board of supervisors has in the selection of grand juries:

Article IX., Section 726.—Grand jurors in each county shall be selected as follows:

The board of supervisors in each county, at least thirty days before each term of a circuit court, shall select twenty persons, to be taken as equally in numbers as may be from each supervisor's district, possessed of the requisite qualifications to serve as grand jurors at the ensuing term.   *   *   *

Section 727.—The names of the person so selected shall be entered on the minutes of the board. The clerk of the board shall, without delay, hand the sheriff of the county a certified copy of such appointment of grand jurors, and the sheriff shall summon such jurors by personal service, if to be found, or, if not, by written notice left at their respective places of abode, at least five days before the commencement of the term, to appear and serve on the grand jury.

It so happens, then, that the grand juries of Kemper county have been, for the past ten years, chosen by democrats. This body of men, after a foreman has been selected by the circuit judge, is placed under the personal supervision of the district attorney, who, in Kemper, has always been a pronounced bourbon and white-liner.

Hence the grand juries have been largely composed of white men, but few negroes being impanneled at any one time. The scarcity of white republicans has sometimes made this a necessity, and afforded a pretext for making a majority of each jury Anglo-Saxon, and favorable to the great tenets of "local self-government." These facts, if nothing else, have often compelled the presiding judge, although a republican, to appoint a foreman from among those entertaining political opinions opposed to his own. Now, with this exhibit before us, it is told that these men have not been indicted, condemned and imprisoned, because, forsooth, "the courts and the juries have been so completely under their control, as to make a conviction for an offense committed by them impossible." Fearing that an enlightened people may not be quite satisfied with a subterfuge like this — and since the courts, juries and everything else have gone into the hands of the "home people," and those who do not agree with them politically, are whipped and murdered without mercy or the hope of justice — a proposition more astounding, and if possible, more hollow and groundless is offered. It is now told that red-handed crime goes unwhipped in Mississippi, because the present "constitution and code of laws were framed and adopted by the republican party, and forced on the people of the State contrary to their will." To give force and credit to this, the genius of the great law dictator of the State, Gen'l J. Z. George is called in, and with a pen ready in all the wiles and deceits of a pettifogging attorney, he puts forth a *State paper* having especial reference to the outlawed condition of society in Kemper county, in which the following language touching the Governor's want of power to enforce the law is used. He says:

That Gov. Stone has not greater powers, is not the fault of the white people of Mississippi. His powers are derived from, and limited by a constitution and *a code of laws which were framed and adopted by the Republican party, and forced on the people of the State contrary to their will.*

The code of laws under which the courts of the State are now operating, was revised by a commission appointed by Governor Alcorn, composed of the following gentlemen: Judge J. A. P. Campbell, Amos R. Johnson and Amos Lovering. The two first named are democrats, and now stand at the head of the bar of the State. It is a fact well known to every school boy, that the criminal code of to-day is the same as that of 1857, save only so far as was made necessary to alter and amend by the requirements of the late amendments to the constitution of the United States relating to slavery. It is almost a *verbatim* copy of that of the State of New York, the code which was originally adopted by the early colonies, and taken from that of the old English laws which have also been received by each succeeding State of the Union since the formation of the government, and stand on all the statute books of the country as they have stood for two hundred years.

It is told, then, that the laws were not enforced against republicans accused of crime, because of the inability of the courts to reach them through the grand juries, the great committing tribunal; and now, that crime under democratic rule stalks abroad in defiance of all law, we are consoled with the announcement, from so high an authority as that of General George, that the statutes are not enforced because *they were thrust upon the people against their will by a republican administration, and in consequence it is not desired that the laws should be enforced.* But this argument is in keeping with the spirit manifested throughout, in a vain endeavor to palliate and cover up a crime too disgraceful and humiliating to be quietly passed over by any people or government claiming rank among the civilized nations, and which the authorities have neither the manhood or the disposition to try to punish. The author quoted, who lives a hundred miles from Kemper county, and who knows nothing whatever of its people, in the same paper alluded to, has another assertion equally erroneous and groundless. Here it is:

To say that these men (meaning the victims of the Kemper tragedy) were killed because they were republicans, and that it is unsafe for a man to proclaim himself a republican in Mississippi, is a gross error.

Strangely in contrast is this with the reasoning of one Robert J. Love, who has been a resident of Kemper county since 1836, and now an old man just tottering to the grave. Mr. Love, from his long and intimate association with the people, ought to be able to speak with some degree of correctness — setting aside, of course, the old man's manifest sympathy for and loyalty to his "county." He says:

I think I know the territory of the county and the people of the county as well as any man living, and I say to-day, take the radical population out of the county and in proportion to numbers, the people of this county have as many good citizens as any county in this State or any other State.

CHAPTER XXIII.

The fact has never been denied that Judge Chisolm and his associates were originally from among the best class living in Kemper at the time. As such they were received and accepted prior to the organization of the party to which in after years they allied themselves. And now the authority of Mr. Love, a venerable citizen, a resident of the county for forty years, is given, who declares that as soon as these men espoused the cause of "radicalism" they became mean and despicable, as no other reason for this sudden transition of character is given. Besides, he says, "take the radical population out of the county" and everybody left in it is found to be good and virtuous.

The two letters quoted from in the preceding chapter one written by General George, who knows nothing of the people of Kemper, and the other by Judge Love, who knows all about them, were both printed in the same issue of the Meridian *Homestead*. One of the writers claims that politics had nothing whatever to do with the massacre at DeKalb, while the other as firmly asserts — with far better grounds of authority — that politics was the primary and only cause of all the trouble had there. The conflicting elements which seem to have dethroned the reasoning faculties of these great writers have seized upon the governor himself; for, on the 4th day of October, 1876, in a letter to Attorney-

General Taft, assuring that functionary of the political and domestic tranquility of the State, Governor Stone wrote as follows:

I am more than willing, and have been able to execute the laws of Mississippi and conserve the public peace. * * The perpetrators of wrongs are responsible to the State authorities, and I am able to bring all such to justice, and am determined to do so.

On the 24th day of May, 1877, but a little more than a year later, just a few days after having visited the scene of the most wanton and appalling outlawry ever committed by beings wearing the human form, His Excellency said:

I have no power to do anything at all. I think it doubtful whether a jury of that county (meaning Kemper) will ever convict one of the mob.

In the face of all these facts the governor, in his annual message of the 2d of January, 1877, addressed to the assembled wisdom of the State—the democratic legislature—is heard in the following language:

It is with feelings of profound pleasure that I congratulate you on the domestic and social prosperity and tranquility of our beloved State. *During the recent exciting political canvass, comparative peace and good order prevailed.* No disturbance was reported that was not promptly met and suppressed by the local authorities, nor has it been charged that any citizen of the State refused to submit to, or in any way resisted the authority of any civil officer. So far as I am advised, not a single disturbance occurred on the day of election; and at no time since the organization of the State Government, have the people been more peaceful, quiet and law-abiding.

In times of "comparative peace" in Mississippi, there is shown a want of respect for the laws, and a lack of energy on the part of the "local authorities" in their execution, which in many of the states of the union where a wholesome fear of the courts is maintained, would at once produce a sense of insecurity to life and property so great, as to call out at once the united voice of the people, for a revision of the code or an immediate change of officers entrusted with its enforcement. Indeed there is a spirit of lawlessness pervading the State, shocking to the better sense of many of its older and better citizens. Scores of men die from violence of one kind or another, year after year, amounting in the aggregate to thousands since the war, and not a solitary white man has been executed during the time. Feuds spring up between individuals and families, collisions occur and deaths follow, and in many cases there is no interference by the "local authorities." At the most, if the offender sees proper to give himself into custody — and there is generally a division of sentiment as to which may be the offender, the murderer or the murdered — he will be placed under a nominal bond, at once released and there the matter to him is virtually at an end, unless a relative or a friend of the deceased, taking the law in his own hands, in turn kills the assassin. It is by no means a rare occurrence for "difficulties" like these spoken of, to be followed up through succeeding generations. One after another the victims fall; children are trained up to avenge the loss of those gone before, and during all the years of bloody sacrifice, not a man involved sees the inside of a prison wall, nor feels the gentle pressure of the elastic hemp. This vengeful thirst — it is said with sorrow — is not always confined to the stronger sex. The writer has seen a pretty girl with white hands, large, dreamy eyes and drooping lashes, one who would cry out horror stricken to see a worm wantonly crushed under foot, on being questioned as to her feelings toward General Ames, the republican governor of the State, (who, with his accomplished wife and interesting family of children lived in the same town with herself,) at once bristle up with an expression as savage as an enraged tigress and exclaim: "I could tear out his tongue and heart and burn him alive!"

The people of the South are governed by passion and prejudice more than by reason or law. This, to many, may sound strangely and even harsh, and when such things are said of woman, it should be done with due regard for the facts, and at the same time with reverence for all those higher and more refining influences which she is admitted to exert over the conduct of men. But when the women of a country, lost to all those tender emotions peculiar to the sex — which are sometimes wanting in men — can contemplate, with cool deliberation, scenes of cruelty which might appall the heart of a Catherine de Medici, then indeed there is little hope for its people.

Neighborhood broils are of frequent occurrence, in which the friends of either party rally upon the streets under arms — generally, though not always, concealed weapons—menacing and threatening each other with instant death, while the "better citizens" and the "local authorities" stand back aghast in momentary expectation of seeing the pavements drenched with blood. To promenade the walks armed, with a double-barrel gun, avowedly for the purpose of "killing on sight" some unfortunate individual, supposed to have been guilty of a breach of etiquette, is a scene which often and again enlivens the monotony of our best regulated towns; and the natural solemnity and grandeur which an act of this kind is sure to inspire, is often made doubly imposing by contrast, when the holy quiet of the Sabbath is called to witness its enactment.

Not many years ago, nor far removed from the city of Jackson, while traveling on one of the railroads leading into that place, a lady, still wearing the widow's weeds, might have been seen to enter one of the coaches, leading by the hand a little boy, six or eight years of age. After taking a seat, her eyes soon became fixed upon a gentleman, well dressed and apparently in the full enjoyment of life and all its attendant blessings, who was sitting in another part of the car. Remaining, with her gaze for a moment upon him, she arose from her seat, still leading the boy, and advancing directly in front of the object of her attention, pointing her finger full in the man's face, in a clear and distinct voice thus addressed her child: "My son, there sits the one who murdered your father!"

What a volume of condemnation and reproach is contained in this brief sentence of that widowed mother;

and what a commentary it is upon a state of society that winks at and tolerates such outrages, and suffers them to go unpunished. How many widows and orphans, made so by the unrestrained hand of violence, there are in Mississippi to-day, God only knows, but they may be counted by tens of thousands.

The State teems with little newspapers; for when the fact is well established that a man is utterly incapacitated for carrying on any legitimate trade or business he is most likely to ascend the tripod, and through the agency of a "patent inside," and the logic of the shotgun, become a dictator of public sentiment and morals. If an editor's credit survives a dozen issues of his sheet, he is entitled, by the law of a long established custom, to *honors* of some kind, and there being nothing else so cheap, a "handle" is at once affixed to his name, and one supposed to be commensurate in "tone" with the number of his subscription list, exclusive of "dead heads." This is the means through which Mississippi gained a large share of its notoriety in the production of "titled" gentry. For the bestowal of these doubtful compliments upon public benefactors, age and length of service very properly take precedence, and we have, first: the "Nestor," "Blucher," or "Sage and Philosopher of the Mississippi press." Then, coming down to more sublunary things, there is presented an array of titles — more commonly applied to military chieftains — in regular gradation, from the rank of "general" down to the humble grade of "captain." The development and flight of genius in the sphere of journalism in Mississippi, in this respect, has been remarkable. It is with pride, however, that a few are excepted from this general rule. There is scarcely an issue of one of these journals that does not contain an account of some act of outlawry, horrifying enough in its details to freeze the blood of a savage. Before me, as I write, lay four different papers of the kind alluded to, all published within one week, in remote and separate parts of the State, and each one reciting the details of a local tragedy, the most heinous and diabolical. And by whom are these murders committed? By men who are at once branded as outlaws and enemies to their race and kind? Not at all! Are they at once hunted down by the officers of the law, backed by an indignant and outraged populace, arrested and confined in jail, there to await speedy trial and execution at the end of the law? No; by no means. Neither are they to be compared with the leaders of the recent terrible riots in the Northern States; their cases are wide apart. The men spoken of here are the aristocrats and leaders of society. They represent the wealth, intelligence and virtue of the communities in which they live. Mechanics, operatives, and ignorant day laborers are not counted among these. They are "gentlemen" of education and too often of leisure, taken from the ranks of the learned professions and the higher walks in life. Teachers, lawyers, doctors, and those who pray loudest in public, if not ministers themselves, are the leaders of riots in Mississippi, and their operations are against the ignorant and defenseless masses; in short, they are "gentlemen," and as such their "dignity" must be respected. Hence it is that in every town and neighborhood may be found more or less men who walk the streets like a very lord, and boast of having "killed their man!" The writer can call to mind nine of the class last named, whom he meets on the street every day. Indeed a newspaper that fails to keep up with the complete details of the numerous tragedies which are being enacted from day to day is deemed wanting in the proper spirit of enterprise, and its patronage falls off.

And all of this in times of "comparative peace," when the issues to be adjusted — if an issue is at stake — are free from political considerations, and exclusively between white men and "gentlemen." At the same time, let a negro be accused of a crime against one of his own race, even, and his punishment, after the most extreme interpretation of the law, will be swift enough; but let the offense be committed by the negro against a white man, and the slow and cumbersome processes of a judicial tribunal are deemed inadequate to meet the demands of palpitating justice, and many times the victim is made to pay the penalty at once, under the lash or the hempen cord, according to the nature of the offense, or rather, according to the height of the "indignation" to be appeased. The will of a single white man is sufficient to procure the arrest and summary punishment of a negro at any time. These things are matters of common observation, when the body politic is in a quiescent state and no direct question of section or race enters into or forms any material part of the subject matter in controversy. But once let an "exciting political canvass" begin, such as the governor faintly alludes to in that portion of his late message above quoted, and such as is here feebly described; then it is that a realization of the facts just enumerated may be felt. When all the bitterness, passion and prejudice engendered by the late war and its results, so disastrous to the material interests of the southern people, and so humiliating to their sectional pride, is aroused to the pitch of frenzy, then it is that "comparisons" become odious when speaking of "domestic tranquility." When the antagonisms existing between the old master and the late slave assume the attitude and alarming proportions of an "irrepressible conflict"; when all these influences are brought to bear, then it is that a light as unmistakable as that afforded by the noon-day sun bursts upon the view, and all the terrifying features of the hydra-headed monster, which the lovers of republican government have to confront, are revealed. However much the more sagacious leaders in the South may strive to conceal the fact, it is nevertheless true, that in each succeeding political contest since the war, the issues have been very closely allied with those which were made the subject of debate and bitter contest at the beginning of that eventful period.

The friends of republicanism meet with the same uncompromising opposition, that union men did in the South in 1860 and 1861, and the stronger the hold which is fastened upon the government, and the greater the number of "Confederate brigadiers" who secure seats in the national congress, the more bitter, persistent and determined seems to be the opposition to everything sought to be introduced and maintained here, that is not democratic in name and southern in principle.

For generations the youth of the country have been educated and trained to spurn the very form of the government under which they lived and prospered for so many years. The same sentiment is fostered and encouraged in their institutions of learning to-day.

The cardinal principles of popular government are too plebeian ever to be appreciated by the high-born sons of the South; and a constitution which places the sturdy men of toil upon an equal footing with themselves in the management and control of national affairs, never has been nor never will be by them cherished and adopted.

Thus, in an "exciting political canvass," there is no such thing as peace, save that peace which is secured by armed and organized opposition to the will of a large and defenseless class, in open defiance of law, justice and humanity—a peace purchased at the alarming sacrifice of the dearest rights known to an American citizen.

CHAPTER XXIV.

The first of August following the massacre at DeKalb, Governor Stone received the nomination of his party, in general convention assembled, for continuance in the responsible position at the time filled by him. On the eleventh of the same month Phil Gully, at a primary canvass in Kemper county, was similarly endorsed for the office of sheriff; and on the sixth of the present month — November — the Governor was re-electd, without opposition, to fill that place of honor and trust; while Gully was defeated by George Welch, the present deputy sheriff, who ran independently.

Already the reward of merit in the realization of a hope long deferred is received, and upon the regal brow of Welch rests the coronet of leadership in his county, while upon Governor Stone are lavished the highest honors within the gift of the whole people.

Thus the first opportunity is improved for returning thanks, in a substantial manner, for the services rendered by these two patriots; one chief among the conspirators and murderers, and the other the chief executive officer of the State, who, in answer to the pathetic appeal of Mrs. Chisolm for aid, "had no power to do anything at all."

Weeks and months dragged their slow length along and no effort was made by any one to apprehend or bring these men to an account. They walked the streets

from day to day, and rode past the homes desolated by
their bloody hands, while the widow and orphan at the
door, in the sable garments of mourning, were made the
subjects of rude and insolent jest. Confident in the
belief that no legal process would ever reach them, or
bring their names in any public way to notice, they
became boastful of the individual gallantry displayed on
the memoral 29th of April, and among themselves and
their admirers there existed a strong rivalry of opinion
as to whom should be awarded the honor of having
been the first, second or third to mount the breach at
the head of the stairs and face that girl, whose white
hands offered the only resistance to their free passage
into the jail. It has already been told that the first one
to enter—Rosser—met the fate he so richly deserved.
Upon another "young man," if we are to believe the
organ whose province is truthfully to represent the sentiments of the people and record passing events, the
Meridian *Mercury*, has been assigned the "third" place
of distinction. The venerable editor of the paper
alluded to, in his notice of this chivalrous scion of a
noble ancestry, through some unaccountable fatality,
neglected to give to the world the name of his hero, but
leaves us with the inference that, from a safe retreat at
the head of the stairs, the "young man" calmly viewed
the field, and was thus enabled to tell all the girl did
"up thare," who, to use his own language, only "run and
screamed and hollered!"

During four long months of masterly inactivity on
the part of the "local authorities," the eyes of the country

were turned upon Mississippi, and the voice of condemnation fell heavily upon the people of the State, standing supinely by, voluntary witnesses of open and undisguised murder in their midst, without the expression of of a desire for the execution of the law. Through the continued cries for justice, there settled upon the hearts of a class not altogether lost to shame or remorse, the feeling that at least the forms of a legal investigation should be observed. This was strengthened and encouraged by their leaders aspiring to political honors, for now the era of reconciliation and good will had come and spread its soft wings over the whole country. The olive branch had been extended to the "erring brethren," who had solemnly plighted their faith to lie down and sleep quietly by the confiding lamb. "Home rule and local self-government" had been guaranteed to them for all coming time, and they were not without the hope of a complete restoration to the old place of power and influence in the political control and management of the government. Already the well-preserved and shapely outlines of the "Lost Cause" which had passed but temporarily from view, could be seen in the no distant future like a bright star cheering them on their lonely pilgrimage. No rash act should be committed now. The cost of a hasty and unguarded step, showing want of sincerity in their professions of good faith could not be estimated, for it might dash to earth the cup so near the famished lips.

Accordingly, the September term of the circuit court for Kemper county was held, when, with a great sound of trumpets, true bills for murder in the first degree were found against six or seven of the leaders in the Chisolm massacre. It was known and well understood in the community for weeks and months before, that the bloodiest of the gang would then be indicted. They themselves knew this to be a part of the programme, and were by no means adverse to such a course, believing that the finding against them would have the effect to satisfy the demand for justice from abroad, and knowing very well that no inconvenience would ever be experienced on account of any further interference by the courts, these villains looked on and viewed this farce with an air of quiet composure, if not absolute delight. The circuit judge had occupied all these months in which to prepare a charge to the grand jury, well calculated in its diction and subject matter to meet the emergency and fall like a soft lullaby song upon the Northern ear. Upon this "masterly paper" the Jackson *Clarion* of October 24th—after copying the "charge" in full—comments as follows:

Judge Hamm's charge to the Kemper county grand jury will be found on our first page. It is an invaluable contribution to the jurisprudence of the State, and, indeed, will form a separate and distinct chapter in its history. No member of society, no matter what his avocation, can fail to be benefited by reading it. It is "profitable for doctrine, for reproof, for correction, for instruction." *The Northern partisan press which, forgetting the beam in its own eyes, have discovered no respect for law and order in Mississippi, will do our State justice and their readers a benefit by copying this masterly paper.*

How it is that the action of these men, sworn to secrecy, has been heralded to the world, after having found six or seven indictments for murder in the first degree, before an arrest or an attempt at arrest has been made, does not appear. The statutes of the State provide that the accused shall be apprehended and confined in jail, *without bail*, there to await trial, and until such time no juryman, without violating a solemn oath, can reveal the secret of their finding. Are not the above facts, taken in connection with the *Clarion's* editorial on Judge Hamm's charge, a sufficient proof to convince the most skeptical of the hollow mockery with which the name of "justice" is clothed in Mississippi? But we are not prepared to stop here with this "Picture of Home Rule." One more brief chapter, however, on Kemper county, and the dark record closes.

In another place it is told that a colored man named Walter Riley was suspected of having killed one Dabbs some years ago. Since then little has been known of the facts or of Riley himself, until just before the assassination of John W. Gully, at which time, it is now said, Riley was seen in the neighborhood of DeKalb; and being unable through all the devilish enginery at their command to fasten the guilt of John W. Gully's untimely taking off upon Rush, thereby making Chisolm accessory to the crime, a new departure is resorted to and a plan, if possible, more diabolical than that of murdering innocent men and women in open day. In the communication of "A Subscriber," elsewhere printed and commented upon —a writer evidently with a prophetic and omnipresent

eye, who reads the thoughts of men with greater ease
and exactness than he could read a book — we are
informed that no negro could have been the assassin of
the great chieftain of their clan; that the crime was committed by a white man who took off his victim's boots
in order to make it appear like the work of some one
who had the object of plunder in view. But here, as in
former chapters, the language of the conspirators themselves is used to fasten the evidence of their guilt upon
them. Riley's relations with Gully are said to have been
of such a nature as to warrant him, at any time — under
the Kemper county code — in taking the life of the latter
whenever an opportunity might offer, and presently it
was whispered about that Riley was the guilty man.
Accordingly, just before the sitting of the court in September last, Riley was kidnapped from Tennessee, where
he had taken refuge, and brought back to Kemper
county, without process of a lawful requisition, or any
other legal authority. But a few days had elapsed
after his arrival before he was convicted of the murder
of Dabbs and sentenced to death; and here follows the
denouement. Riley was to have been hanged on the 9th
of November following his condemnation. Meantime,
Phil Gully and his associates had free access to the
prisoner's cell, and from time to time, it is well known,
the condemned man was approached with the promise
of a commutation of sentence, or a reprieve, if he would
only say that he was the one who killed John W. Gully,
and that it was done at the instigation of Chisolm and
others. It is now said that Riley has confessed to

having killed Gully, believing himself justifiable in so doing, but, in the face of death, has steadily refused to say that any other man, living or dead, was cognizant of the fact.

Meantime, it is told, that three different attempts have been made to burn the jail and every one in it. The 9th of November came, and the victim, Riley, was about to be led to the gallows through an immense throng of "good citizens," who had turned out to "hear his confession" or to see him "dangle," when, lo! and behold, a respite of thirty days comes from his Excellency, the Governor! Thus thirty days' more time is given the Gullys, through their attorney, Mr. Woods, and the kind offices of the Governor, in which to devise means to wring from Riley a confession of the guilt of Judge Chisolm, whose martyred remains have long since become food for worms. As these pages go to press —November 24th—it is difficult to tell what may be the final result of this last and most damnable of all the murderous conspiracies which the history of Kemper county civilization furnishes proof.

Seven months have passed since the slaughter of April was committed, and three since the murderers were indicted, and they walk the streets as freely and unconcerned as they did before the sitting of the great tribunal of justice, the circuit court. The newspapers of the South, like the *Clarion*, are loud in their praises of Judge Hamm and the "good people" of Kemper for upholding "the majesty of the law," and it is now claimed that northern vandalism against the good name and intent of our "erring brethren," must forever cease. Possibly this is said with a degree of plausibility and even in good faith. If so, it is certainly wrong to "stir up," by unjust criticism, the old wounds of distrust, which the gangrene of sectional pride and jealousy have kept open for so many years. A charitable view leads one to the adoption of this theory; and we are about to bend in humble reverence and submission to its teachings, when the eye, already wet with penitential tears, falls accidentally upon a paragraph in the Meridian *Mercury*, like this, and the dream of restored confidence vanishes like the "baseless fabric of this vision." Hear the *Mercury* once more:

Imagination fails to conceive of anything better calculated to turn the county over to riot and bloodshed than the indictment of one, or two, or many, for a crime committed by a great number of people acting together, and who have boldly stood up to their acts, neither hiding nor shirking the responsibility. They put out of the way men who, for a long series of years, had made a mockery of that justice we have seen so efficiently administered for the last two weeks, and who had made murder and assassination safe in the county from the law's retribution, under the maddening provocation of an assassination they held themselves responsible for, and yet hold them. If it appear that these indictments have been procured to appease a northern public sentiment, and to gratify any home prejudices, we may expect the demon to be awakened again in these people now so calm and acquiescent in the law, and we may dread the result.

The ministers of the law always make a mistake when they assume that the law is to be pushed straight through to the letter, under all circumstances, regarding nothing. That sort of a mistake we fear the Kemper grand jury is making.

The writer of the above is well known to the author of this book, and it is no more than justice to him here o state, in this editorial he utters the honest convictions of his heart. That he speaks the sentiments of the people generally there is no better proof needed than to know that for many long years he has been supported in this style of journalism; that, meantime, his paper has grown in power and influence, and while pursuing this undeviating course touching these grave questions — consistent at least in being straightforward — the *Mercury* has lived to see a half dozen more liberal organs spring up in the same town and die for want of patronage. We have not only this proof of its endorsement by the people, but its editor was last summer at the State convention, which met in Jackson the first of August, a prominent candidate for lieutenant-governor.

But to this day it will be denied that there exists, or ever existed in Mississippi, an ungovernable element now familiarly styled "Bulldozers;" a class of men as formidable in numbers as they are brutal in instinct, disregarding alike the laws of God and man. Many of our incredulous friends at the North are impressed with the truthfulness of this denial. Here is an extract from the Liberty *Herald*, published some time in August or September last, headed " Bulldozing." It may throw a ray of light upon this subject:

We have been asked more than once why, as a public journalist, we have not, through our columns, opposed and denounced in befitting terms the lawlessness which, under the above significant term, is rapidly destroying the material interest of our county and surrounding sections, and bringing us, as a community, into public seandal and disgrace. Our answer has heretofore been, we were ashamed to give any more notoriety to the matter than it already had, and we trusted that a healthy public sentiment would silently but successfully and speedily suppress it. But it seems we were mistaken. It is not only as rampant as ever, but is steadily increasing in the diabolism of its acts and the audacity of its demands. Public sentiment, although opposed to it, is silent, while its advocates are noisy, blatant and organized.

This is followed by an article from the Vicksburg *Herald ;* for now that this great evil is falling heaviest upon those who have been most persistent heretofore in denying its existence, the "laugh"—so to speak—is "on the other side :"

All our citizens feel that there is something wrong in regard to the protection of life and property in our midst, but many do not know where the cause lies. There is a well defined feeling that too many crimes are committed; that too many people are shot or cut, or assaulted with deadly weapons, and that there is too much bummerism and bulldozing of one sort and another. We feel that we are drifting along, and that the lawless are not restrained or promptly punished.

Again His Excellency, the Governor, has been forced to acknowledge the virtue found in the old adage, "It makes a difference whose ox is gored."

Contrast his language of May, in answer to Mrs. Chisolm's appeal, when he had "no power to do any-

thing at all," with that of September last, in answer to
the call of his own distressed brethren.   Here is his
language of the latter date:

EXECUTIVE DEPARTMENT, }
JACKSON, MISS., Sept. 8, 1877. }

Hon. A. C. McNAIR, Brookhaven, Miss.:

Dear Sir: I have the honor to acknowledge receipt
of your favor of —— instant, detailing the condition of
affairs in three of the counties of southwest Mississippi.
I am now in correspondence with leading citizens in
those localities, with a view of ascertaining what the
emergency demands, and then to determine what lawful
means to adopt to meet that emergency.

*Such a state of things cannot be tolerated, and cost
what it may, it must and shall be stopped.*

Yours very truly,

J. M. STONE.

CHAPTER XXV.

Of the "Chisolm Massacre," the names of its active participants are still unknown to the outside world. Unwilling that they should be lost to posterity, a list of those most deserving of notice is furnished below:

Henry Gully,
Phil H. Gully,
Bill Gully,
Jess Gully,
Houston Gully,
Virgil Gully,
Slocum Gully,
John Gully, (Phil's son,)
—— Gully, (Phil's son,)
Jere Watkins,
Dan McWhorter,
Jim Overstreet,
Robt J. Moseley,
James H. Brittain,
Willie Brittain,
Tom Lang,
John H. Overstreet,
John Hunter,
Jim Wanen,
Sloke Wanen,
Sam Wanen,
Baxter Camel,
John Camel,
—— Hodge,
Sanford Jordan,

Jim McRory.
Charles L. McRory,
John T. Gewen,
Tom P. Bell,
Arch Adams,
Bill Adams,
John Adams,
Dr. Stennis,
Dr. Camel,
Jim Whittle,
Robt Waddle,
Pat J. Scott,
J. W. Lang,
Doland Coleman,
Wallace Morrison,
Peck Vandevender,
George Hull,
Philander Hull,
Jess Hull,
—— Shot,
George Eldridge,
Bill Clark,
Foote McLellan,
Dee McLellan,
John Bounds,

Ed Davis,
Bill Williams,
Joe Ellerby,
Joe Hodge,
Rufus Bounds,
Ruff Turner,
Albert Lilly,
Frank Hawin,
Sam Hawin,
Jim Scott,
—— Ivory,
J. J. Hall,
—— Jenkins,
Theodore Clark,
—— McWilliams,
Ebb Felton,
W. J. Overstreet,
Bob Goodwin,
Ed Weston.

Of these, Phil Gully, John J. Overstreet, Sam and Frank Hawin are each indebted to the estate of Judge Chisolm in sums ranging from five dollars up to one hundred and thirty. Tom Bell represents the county in the State Legislature. Ed Weston is coroner and ranger. J. L. Spinks, the justice of the peace whose name illumes so many of the preceding pages, was promoted at the November election to succeed Bell in the house of representatives.

Let these names, in golden letters, be hung up along all the public avenues leading into the State. To the weary immigrant who may chance to turn, in the future, for a home in the soft, genial clime of Mississippi, they will appear like the terrifying warning inscribed against an entrance into Dante's ideal hell, "All hope abandon ye when enter here."

Let them be placed in the capitol at Washington; they will inspire the "gifted Lamar" to honeyed words of reconciliation. The Hon. Mr. Money, when he rises in the seat allotted to the member from the third congressional district of Mississippi, will point with pride to the names of his constituency who carried him through the blood of the murdered Chisolm and his sweet girl and boy, against an honest majority of more than four thousand votes in the district, thus opposed to him, to a place among the nation's great men.

CHAPTER XXVI.

In the face of all the disparaging truths which these pages have recorded, and while the cold rains of December are drenching the graves of the martyred dead, it is a source of gratification to know that the heart of the people has never ceased to beat in the fond hope of justice and the Nemesis yet to come.

American womanhood is everywhere aroused to a sense of that deep shame which overshadows and mocks at our boasted chivalry, so long as the blood of Cornelia Chisolm is unavenged. The talent of the best writers has been employed in condemnation of this crime, and in utter execration of the depraved condition of society which suffers it to go unpunished. To the pen of Grace Greenwood, the Washington correspondent of the New York *Times*, a double debt of gratitude is due. This writer, from the first, has been unremitting in her endeavors to place the matter, in all its enormities, fairly before the people. Others have moulded into verse, a more graceful and touching tribute to the memory of the dead.

A letter printed in the New York *Tribune* the latter part of May following the massacre, touching the subject of the erection of a monument in honor of the heroism of Miss Cornelia Chisolm, full of thought and well worthy the consideration of the "young men of the country" is here appended. It is in response to a suggestion which first appeared in the Indianapolis *Journal*, and is worth a place in these pages:

A MONUMENT TO MISS CHISOLM.

YOUNG MEN SHOULD ERECT IT — WHAT ITS SIGNIFICANCE WOULD BE.

To the Editor of the Tribune:

SIR: The suggestion which has been made by a Western paper that the ladies of the country should erect a monument over the grave of Cornelia Chisolm is one that should not be overlooked. If surprising courage in a sex which Nature has not formed for scenes calling for physical courage; if self-devotion, if filial affection, if all that is most beautiful in woman deserves to be honored, then this generation should see to it that it commemorates the sublime manifestation of these qualities in that young girl. I have read no incident in the history of my country, from the landing of the Pilgrims down to the close of the last war — which was illustrious in deeds of individual heroism — that has so thrilled me with admiration for the individual, or has so elevated my ideas of womanhood, and, I may say, of my kind, as that struggle of Cornelia Chisolm against the murderers of her father. Nay, I defy any one to point out, in the annals of the past, any exhibition of high qualities which is more worthy of the world's reverence than this. The scene has already passed into history; it should be, and I doubt not it will be, commemorated by art, and it should receive the homage of a generation which she honored and for which she died.

But why should women raise this memorial? Let it rather be a tribute of the young men of this country to womanhood, whose highest qualities Cornelia Chisolm

SACRED
TO THE
MEMORY
OF
CORNELIA J. CHISOLM
WHO
DIED
MAY 15TH 1877,
A MARTYR TO
FILIAL LOVE
AND PATRIOTIC DEVOTION.

so strikingly illustrated. Let them show that the manhood of this country honors woman's affection, which shrinks at no sacrifice or danger to protect the object around which it clings, and does not band together to shoot down an innocent girl who throws herself between her father and a murderous mob. And more, let such a memorial tell a debased civilization around it of a manhood which spares weakness and does not crush it; which respects sex and does not make woman's helplessness the measure of its own courage; which honors filial affection and does not make it a pretext for murder; which honors heroism and does not assassinate it; which reverences sublime self-devotion and does not put bloody hands upon it; which has regard for innocence and law, and does not band together to trample upon both. Let it be thus at once a vindication of the manhood of this country, which has been shamed by an outbreak of local brutality, and the proclaimer of a true chivalry in a region where bloodthirsty ferocity, undignified by any noble sentiment, usurps its name.

There is yet another reason why this monument should be reared by the young men of this country. It will be a menace as well as a memorial. Telling of what in human nature they reverenced most, and forming a silent protest against the dishonor with which it has met, it will suggest, inevitably, that there are arms which will be raised to avenge such outrages against what they regard as a sacred thing. A civilization which tolerates, defends and practices the murder of innocent women as a means of political intimidation, has no right to exist upon God's fair earth. Neither constitutional nor prescriptive right will stand before the outraged moral sense of mankind. The Turk is being driven out of Europe, and the turk must be crushed down in America. Let such a memorial as I have advocated speak in Mississippi this voice of the people, which, in this case, is the voice of God. Let it proclaim, that if that murderous civilization shows no signs of improvement, there is a power in this country which, in the fullness of time, will grind it to powder. REDINGTON.

Below is reproduced a beautiful poem, by Mary Clemner, read last summer on the occasion of the celebration of our Natal Day, in one of the northern cities. This is followed by others, which have come to the notice of the author, during the progress of this work. The poems cannot fail to add interest to its pages, as they must certainly touch the hearts of all who read them:

> What do we celebrate?
> Freedom's new birth　Elate
> While on the sad East's verge,
> The sullen war waves surge,
> And lines of battle break
> In blood, "for Christ's dear sake?"
> Our bells of Freedom ring,
> Our songs of Peace we sing;
> And do we dream we hear
> The far, low cry of fear,
> Where in the Southern land,
> The masked, barbaric band,
> Under the covert night,
> Still fight the coward's fight.
> Still strike the assassin's blow,
> Smite childhood, girlhood low?
> Great Justice! canst thou see
> Unmoved that such things be?
> See murderers go free,
> Unsought?　Bruised in her grave
> The girl, who fought to save
> Brother and sire.　She died for man.
> She leads the lofty van
> Of hero women.　Lift her name
> With ever-kindling fame.
> Her youth's consummate flower
> Took on the exalted dower
> Of martyrdom.　And Death,
> And Love put on her crown
> Of high renown.　*　*　*

Johnny Mann Chisolm

Cease, bells of Freedom, cease!
Hush, happy songs of Peace!
If such things yet may be,
"Sweet land of Liberty,"
In thee, in thee!
On hill top and in vale
Lie low our brethren pale,
June roses on each breast,
Beloved! ye are blest!
Ye yielded up your breath,
Ye gave yourselves to death,
For Freedom's sake. We live
To see her wounds. We live
To bind her wounds. To give
Life up for her high sake,
If life she need. We take
The Cross that ye laid down.
The world may smile or frown,
We kiss the sacred host,
We count the priceless cost,
We swear in holy pain,
O! sacrificial slain,
Ye did not die in vain!

"LITTLE JOHNNY."

BY W. S. PETERSON.

Softly breathed the coming May
On that Southern Sabbath day.

In that genial, sunny clime
May days come before their time.

Earth and sky were bright and blest
On the holy day of rest.

But no sound of prayer and psalm
Rose upon the Sabbath's calm.

And the morning sun looked down
On a mob-beleaguered town.

Horsemen galloped here and there,
And their curses filled the air.

Soon a hundred ruffians yell
Round the home where heroes dwell.

Brave Judge Chisolm scorning fear
Though the wolves of hell were near;

And Cornelia, heroine rare,
Fair and young and brave as fair;

Little Johnny, aged thirteen,
Bravest boy the world has seen!

When the Judge to jail was led,
" I'll go too! " brave Johnny said.

Sire and son walked hand in hand
Through the threat'ning ruffian band.

And within the prison gate
Johnny shared his father's fate.

When the mob, with savage yell
On their helpless victims fell,

Johnny stood and faltered not
In the furious storm of shot—

Stood beside his sister there
On the splintered, bloody stair —

Held the door, and kept at bay
Fiends who would his father slay,

Till the leader of the band
Shot away his little hand!

Then, to save his sire from harm,
He stretched out his shattered arm,

Sprang before the powder flame
That toward his father came,

And received in his own form
The full fury of the storm,

Till his body, torn with lead,
At his father's feet fell dead!

*　　*　　*　　*　　*　　*

When he to his grave was borne,
Few there were for him to mourn.

Mississippi, murder-wild,
Mourned not for her noblest child.

Not a hymn or prayer was heard,
Priest nor preacher spoke a word.

Only she who gave him birth
Sigh'd the sad words, "Earth to Earth."

Only his own mother wept
Where her darling hero slept.

But his little grave shall yet
With a Nation's tears be wet.

And through all the coming years,
With their eyes bedimmed by tears,

Mothers to their sons shall tell
How heroic Johnny fell.

Storied page and poet's song
Shall his praises still prolong;

And while Love and Valor live,
Men to Johnny's name shall give

The first place on history's page
With the heroes of the age.

JOHNNY CHISOLM, AGED THIRTEEN,
BRAVEST BOY THE WORLD HAS SEEN!

OUR HEROINE.

DEDICATED TO MRS. JUDGE CHISOLM.

In all the tears that woman can shed,
With all the sympathy that woman can give.

Into the precinct of thy heart,
Where pierceth deep the poignant dart,
We would not penetrate,
E'en to uproot the pang. 'T were vain,
Since husband, daughters, sons are slain
God only can remove the sting.
Unto Him all thine offerings bring.

With feelings all akin to those
Felt when we read of Him who rose
Triumphant from the grave,
Would we, as if in solid rock,
Write the one universal thought,
Our heroine died to save.

Inspired forever be thy kind,
To nobler deeds and loftier mind,
    Our murdered heroine.
Proud freedom's cause was on the wane ;
It springeth to new life again.
    Be all the glory thine.

Untrammeled by earth's lesser aims,
Unfettered, free from all its pains,
    Thy spirit lingereth nigh.
It woos us e'en to bravery,
To die for right, if need there be,
    Avenged! thy death we cry.

" Vengeance is mine; I will repay ;"
As in the past is ours to-day ;
    The edict is his own.
Beside Joan of Arc in fame,
We place in mem'ry thy dear name.
    Martyred Cornelia Chisolm.

Mrs. W. F. Lutz.

CHAPTER XXVII.

In the characters whose lives form the important features of this work, are presented a considerable number of men whose rights and immunities as citizens of a common country entitled them, at the outset, to equal consideration and respect with any other class.

Alienation of birth or distinction of caste was not made a pretext for marking them in any way as objects of distrust, derision or contempt. Their daily conduct did not differ materially from that of the better people with whom they were associated. No conventionalities, no prejudices incident to religious belief, race or condition singled them from their fellows. Natives of the soil from which their sustenance was drawn, the interests of these men were identical with those of others among whom their life fortunes were fixed. That unfortunate genius to whose villainy is ascribed all the mischief and crime committed in the Southern states since the surrender, was not found among them. No one had a better right to judge of the wants of the community or to devise means for supplying its demands than they. No "*vile carpet-bagger*" ever polluted the sacred soil where the scenes of this story are laid. But as time advances the onward tide of thought keeps pace. In passing, truths are gathered up and errors cast off by the wayside, old land marks are swept away and new theories in science, art and statesmanship are adopted. In the course of years, emerging from a great national convulsion, which in its results is said to have solved the problem of human bondage on the American continent and settled forever all the vexed questions growing out of its existence, we find in Kemper county, the class of men above alluded to, have honestly accepted the situation and in common with all good citizens undertaken to live and act in compliance with the requirements of the constitution and its late amendments. Against these are arrayed those who have made the overthrow of the Republic and the principles upon which it was reared, the one great crowning object of their lives. The one, actuated by a sense of duty, struggle to maintain the supremacy of the law and the perpetuity of republicanism; the other, blinded by sectional jealously and trained in a school of hatred to every principle of popular government, moved by the spirit which inspired them in 1861, are still worshiping the god of rebellion and disunion.

Following the picture to its close, we find the former overpowered by organized and armed opposition, humbled, beaten and subjected; their leaders slain and their ranks broken and thinned by the assassin's bullet; while the latter, jubilant and defiant, conscious of their ability to defeat the ends of justice, and dead to human sympathy, laugh at every effort to bring them to an accountability of their great crimes.

On a little plateau overlooking the village of DeKalb, not more than one hundred and fifty yards distant from its business centre, stands the Chisolm cottage. At its front door and windows the widowed mother watches for the return of her two little boys, who, with the rising sun leave the house for the plantation three miles distant, where their time is employed in the endeavor to secure a crop with which to discharge the pressing obligations of the estate. At evening, when listening for their returning steps, the coarse laugh and loud curses of drunken revelers at the Gully grocery and other kindred places, are wafted to her ears. In these voices she recognizes the men whose blood-stained hands have desolated her hearth-stone, and robbed her of husband and children. At every sound of pistol or gun, trembling with fear, the anxious mother looks out, ever conscious of the danger which threatens the older boy, Clay, whose advancing years have already made him an object for the attention of his father's murderers.

Every officer of the county, with perhaps one or two exceptions, and through whose hands the business of the Chisolm estate must pass in settlement, either participated in the slaughter of April last, or are in active sympathy with those who did. Charlie Rosenbaum, the only willing and competent man in the county who knows anything about the late Judge's business affairs, under repeated threats of assassination, compelled to abandon his own business at Scooba, where, at the time of the DeKalb massacre he was a prosperous merchant, is powerless to render the assistance so much needed. While Southern statesmen of the Kemper school are gaining admission to the highest places in the national councils, the "bloody shirt" by common consent of their Northern co-laborers, is sneeringly held up as a vulgar and unclean thing. Meantime Mrs. Chisolm, through the dark hours of her desolation, turns from her lonely watch at the windows to the pictures of her murdered darlings, and weeps as only a wife and mother crushed and bruised, can do. Leaving the portraits, with a dead heart she turns to the room once her daughter's, still ornamented with the touch of her deftly fingers. There stands her piano, its mute keys unmoved since that brave right hand was struck by the assassin's bullet. There on the walls are Cornelia's first girlish efforts at art, placed in humorous contrast with those of a more mature date. In a corner are laid away the keepsakes and playthings of her happy childhood, only just passed. Turning from these, the mother goes softly and silently to the wardrobe where is carefully placed the clothing worn by her loved ones on that dark Sabbath of April 29. The first article that greets her tear-dimmed eyes is Cornelia's little hood, with the strings shot off and stained with blood. Then her clothing, from the neck to the feet clotted with gore and perforated with bullets, not even the shoes escaping the leaden charge. The shattered bracelet and the ball which passed through her arm, with the yellow metal clinging to its battered surface, next appear. Then Johnny's shirt, with the sleeve shot off, charred with burning gunpowder, and the hole in the left breast, four inches broad, where his heart's blood oozed out. Turning, the tattered garments of Judge Chisolm, containing blood enough to "incarnadine the multitudinous seas," are found on the other hand. There, apart from civilization, shut out from all friendly intercourse, menaced, and her little boy, at the very hour of this writing, driven to the woods for safety; alone and without hope of relief, the patriot widow lives on.